Mustard Seed Thoughts

FRESH FAITH AND NEW LIFE

BOOK 1 - KEY TO LIFE

With many thanks!

Anita E. Keire

Anita E. Keire

CURRICULUM DEVELOPMENT ASSOCIATES, INC.

Curriculum Development Associates, Inc.

Greenwich, CT 06830-3027

www.mustardseedseries.com

ISBN: 978-0-9989106-8-0 Print Book

ISBN: 978-0-9989106-9-7 eBook

Library of Congress Control Number: 2020916898

Curriculum Development Associates, Inc.

Greenwich, CT

Library of Congress Cataloging-in-Publication Data

Keire, Anita E.

Christian History

Christian Theology

Christian Apologetics

Christian Inspiration

Christian Self Help

Christian Personal Growth

No Christian would deny that Christ is greater than the theological systems in which men have attempted to expound His significance. We read of Jesus in the gospels that surrounded once by a crowd who wanted to do Him violence, 'He passed through the midst of them and went His way'. So it is with the established Christian orthodoxies. In so far as they want to take Him by force and imprison Him within the boundaries of a particular point of view, Christ eludes them and goes His way. For He belongs everywhere and will be confined nowhere.

— H. A. WILLIAMS, *THE TRUE WILDERNESS*

ALSO BY ANITA E. KEIRE

Walking on Water: Skeptics and Believers Discuss Whether Jesus Matters

Resurrection Dialogues with Skeptics and Believers

A Parent's Guide to Prayer

Mustard Seed Series Director's Book

Mustard Seed Series Teacher's Training Manual

Mustard Seed Series Kindergarten Teacher Book

Mustard Seed Series Kindergarten Student Book

Mustard Seed Series Primary 1 Teacher Book

Mustard Seed Series Primary 1 Student Book

Mustard Seed Series Primary 2 Teacher Book

Mustard Seed Series Primary 2 Student Book

Mustard Seed Series Intermediate 1 Teacher Book

Mustard Seed Series Intermediate 1 Student Book

Mustard Seed Series Intermediate 2 Teacher Book

Mustard Seed Series Intermediate 2 Student Book

Mustard Seed Series Junior 1 Teacher Book

Mustard Seed Series Junior 1 Student Book

Mustard Seed Series Junior 2 Teacher Book

Mustard Seed Series Junior 2 Student Book

Mustard Seed Series Pre-Confirmation 1 Teacher Book

Mustard Seed Series Pre-Confirmation 1 Student Book

Mustard Seed Series Pre-Confirmation 2 Teacher Book

Mustard Seed Series Pre-Confirmation 2 Student Book

Mustard Seed Series Confirmation Teacher Book

Mustard Seed Series Confirmation Student Book

See sample chapters on www.mustardseedseries.com and/or on Amazon.com.

ACKNOWLEDGMENTS

Many thanks go to the Letters Women of the Greenwich, CT, Branch of the National League of American Pen Women who critiqued and offered helpful advice and encouragement in the creation of *Mustard Seed Thoughts: Fresh Faith and New Life.*

CONTENTS

Introduction   xi

1. A Starting Point   1
2. The Bible   5
3. Early Genesis Stories   9
4. Why Work?   13
5. Choices   19
6. Endings   25
7. The Neutral Zone   29
8. A Family Affair   33
9. Forgiveness and Reconciliation   37
10. Meeting God   41
11. Excuses, Excuses   47
12. Are Holy Wars Legitimate?   53
13. Just War Theory   61
14. Where is God?   69
15. Longings   73
16. Validation   79
17. A Brief History from Moses to Jesus   81
18. High Hopes   85
19. God's Love is Vulnerable   93
20. Why Does God Allow Evil to Exist?   97
21. Rejection   101
22. Why the Slaughter   111
23. A Call to Action   117
24. John the Baptist, Jesus' Baptism and Temptations   121
25. Jesus Begins His Ministry   127
26. Are You A Religious Skeptic?   131
27. How Do You Handle Worldly Temptations?   137
28. Some Everyday Spiritual Challenges   143
29. Wounded Healers   167
30. The Gift of Life   171

31. Trust   175
32. Why Jesus Is Called the Suffering Servant   181

   Afterword   187

INTRODUCTION

This series of books are written to give you a fresh look at religious beliefs and whether they are still valid for you today.

For you, it may be as unpredictable as crossing the wide Atlantic Ocean where you will encounter raging storms, calm seas and smooth sailing.

Doubt is part of my faith journey. I have always questioned boiler plate answers to challenging beliefs especially when head winds made me change my course in life. I believe that only through a personal understanding of our Christian beliefs and our struggle with our doubts can we come to enjoy the conviction necessary to make a thoughtful commitment to God and the Christian way of life. If we allow the Kingdom of God to grow within us as the lowly mustard seed, and if we fertilize and water it so that it can grow and mature, we will have an enduring faith that grows out of knowledge and love of God.

You may also have experienced some troubling thoughts and unanswered questions in your spiritual journey on the high seas of your passage through life. In these books, I want to share with you my struggles, thoughts, and beliefs. Maybe my years in Christian ministry and insights learned may be of some help to you in the forthcoming chapters and books yet to be written. So, join me on a voyage of discovery and glean what you can from it. Be prepared to be challenged and possibly to disagree with me. You may wish to have your friends and family accompany you on this journey as well.

> Jesus calls us, o'er the tumult
> Of our life's wild restless sea;
> Day by day his voice stills calls us,
> Saying 'Christian, follow me.'

— Cecil F. Alexander 1818-1895

A STARTING POINT

THE SCRAPING sounds of the front double doors and the outside storm doors being forced open in the wintry night awake me. I can hear people talking ever so quietly in the front hall. My older sister in the bed beside me sleeps on. The time I have prayed for and against is now. I know my mother is dead. Her pain and her three-year battle with cancer are over.

I am 11 years old. The next few days are busy with funeral preparations, family, and friends. Then my father, three brothers, two sisters and I are by ourselves. Platitudes such as "She was too good to live" and "God took her home" were people's well-meaning efforts to comfort me and to answer my questions: "Why did she get sick?" "Why did she suffer?" "Why did she have to die?" "Why did God take her away?" "Where is she now?" "Where or what is heaven?" These questions haunted me for years. I never questioned the existence of God, only people's expectations of and explanations about God.

I remember a special trip I made to my father's office to ask him specific questions about my mother's death. I wanted to be alone with him and to hear from him where my mother was. He listened not too patiently. Looking back after these many years, no doubt his grief and doubts were just as great as my own. The difference was that he had the maturity to know that doubt is often a partner of belief. For me, his abbreviated answers lacked clarity. I did not understand what he told me, and he gave me no opportunity for questions and discussion. That is when I decided to keep my questions and doubts about God to myself. I moved to the sidelines and waited for a meaningful dialogue to begin.

When I became old enough to leave home, I did. I went from a small town in Northwest New Jersey to San Francisco. After establishing residency, I entered the University of California at Berkeley. There my intellectual world burst wide open. For the first time in my life, I learned about different world views in a pluralistic environment. I examined the worthiness of these perspectives. From then on I realized that our beliefs about God, acceptance or rejection of different modes of knowing, and the impact of culture and science on our consciousness, all shape our religious sensibilities.

When my daughter entered seventh grade, I accepted the position of Director of Christian Education in an Episcopal Church. This job was a high-water mark in my life. It helped change my views regarding women in the ministry. Parishioners responded to and affirmed my leadership gifts. My experience as daughter, wife, mother, and English teacher prepared me well, but not well enough. I lacked proper theological education that could unwittingly distort the Christian gospel. Self-education was barely meeting the increasing demands expected of me. A church member suggested that I audit some classes at Yale Divinity School. And so I did. What amazed me was the number of women my age in attendance who were seeking ordination. So I listened to my inner call to become a minister. I resigned my position and enrolled as a full-time student at Yale University's Divinity School.

My decades-old questions only raised more questions. This book and future books in this series will reflect on my thoughts on my spiritual journey. The Bible has been and will continue to be my guide in living the Christian life.

Unfortunately, many religious historians, theologians, and authors influence the Christian church's agenda. Some may be undeclared atheists, Gnostics, ideologues, or opportunists who capitalize on people's biblical and theological ignorance and vulnerability. Their impact on religious leaders, lay teachers, and believing individuals may create doubt, tension, and unreflective, uncritical acceptance of many Christian and not-so-Christian beliefs. Part of my struggle, and no doubt yours, has been to discern whose position can be trusted.

THE BIBLE

ONE STUMBLING block for many people is how the Old and New Testament Bible came into existence and why it is considered Holy Scripture for Christians.

Both the Old and New Testaments developed along similar lines. But the Old Testament took a much longer time to develop. They both began as an oral tradition.

Many of the stories we find in the Old Testament were memorized, told, and retold by illiterate tribal storytellers for at least 1,000 years before they were put into writing. That means that these oral stories began some 4,500 years ago.

After the Jewish people entered the Promised Land and after King David had defeated the Philistines, peace made it possible for the people to live in cities and towns. The old tribal system that existed before King David was beginning to fall apart. Their storytellers were beginning to die, and few new storytellers were coming along to replace them.

Because King David was concerned that these Bible stories would be lost forever, he hired scribes to travel into the countryside where the tribal storytellers lived. The scribes wrote down every story that the various storytellers knew about their people.

The process of putting these stories into written form began around the year 950 BCE (before the Common Era or B.C.). It took another 200 years for the Jewish people to collect, combine/merge/edit, and piece together all existing stories into one story.

After this time period, we have additional books written for or by various prophets.

Canon refers to the books selected to be in the Bible. The Old Testament books had to be judged as to their truth and spiritual value. After the fall and destruction of Jerusalem in 70 CE (Common Era or A.D.), the Pharisees concentrated on collecting all known books. Then they held the Council of Jamnia in 90 CE to decide which books should be considered Jewish Holy Scripture and the books that form our Old Testament and their Holy Scripture.

New Testament writings began sometime after 46 CE with the letters of Paul. Before Paul's letters, the gospel message was oral. Very little was in written format. The gospel of Mark is the oldest of the four gospels and was believed to have been written between 64 and 75 CE. This time period includes the war and the destruction of the Temple. The gospel of John was the last one written. It could have been written as early as 90 CE and as late as 120 CE.

Even though the process of developing the New Testament was much shorter and covered events that happened in less than 100 years (as compared to more than 2,000 years for the Old Testament), both the Old and New Testaments went through the same process from Oral Tradition to Written Form, then Collected and Edited to become the Christian Canon.

In 382 CE, the Council of Rome made the final decision as to which gospels, books, and letters were accepted into what is now our New Testament. For instance, the gospel of Thomas was not included in our New Testament because it did not meet the criteria of being widely used and did not represent the beliefs of most Christians. The three main criteria for the acceptance of writings into the New Testament were as follows:

1. *Apostolic origin*—an apostle wrote or authorized the materials to be written.

2. *Fidelity to apostolic teachings*—the contents reflected as nearly as possible apostolic teaching.

3. *Catholicity*—that is, extent of use—extended acceptance and use of the particular materials in many of the early Christian communities.

Some other considerations for the works included in the Bible were *inspiration, authority,* and *canon.*

4. *Inspiration* alone was too broad a category. The Council assumed all documents under consideration were by inspired authors. Therefore, inspiration was an insufficient reason for canonization.

5. *Authority* and *canon* shaped the final form of the Bible. Authority went before the canon; i.e., Paul claimed to be an "Apostle to the Gentiles", inspired by the Holy Spirit, which granted him authority in his dealings with God's churches. Also the church itself held the authority to decide what books would be part of the *canon.*

Throughout the centuries, prophesy continued through other writers. Their works did not become canonical, because they did not meet these first three criteria.

The early church never claimed that God dictated the Bible. To the early church, the Bible was a collection of writings anchored in history and brought together into a canon by a thoroughly historical process. The power of the New Testament writings rested in their status as the expression of other people's experiences, prayers, and revelations with and about God. The wording of the Bible in every instance depended on the decisions of authors and/or editors.

In canonizing certain writings, the Christian church acknowledges them and empowers them to set the norm for faith and life; they would be the criteria by which the church would gauge its faithfulness. In creating the canon, the church subjected itself to these writings as its standard.

The Bible—both Old and New Testaments—is multilayered faith literature. It is the end product of a long and complex history spanning thousands of years. Many cultures affected it, and in its final form it reflects a wide variety of backgrounds and situations.

Think About It

- What are your thoughts about how the Bible came into being?
- Why or why not would you give the Old Testament scripture the same authority as the New Testament?

3

EARLY GENESIS STORIES

ATHEISTS AND AGNOSTICS respond to my beliefs as naïve and misguided. They point to the stories found in Genesis 1-11 as unhistorical, unscientific, pure fiction, and unreliable. They say these stories parallel other creation, flood, and disobedience stories existing in ancient Mesopotamia. That is true. Yet I think these atheists and agnostics miss the point and lack understanding on why these stories exist in the form they are presented and why they are part of Jewish and Christian sacred scripture. They need to understand that these stories are statements of faith and not history or science. Their authors used poetic license to convey the truths about our human condition. To gain spiritual insight, we need to study the motivation and conviction of the people featured throughout scripture.

For instance, Genesis 1 written around 500 BCE is a statement of faith against the worldview of the Babylonians under whom the Jewish people lived in forced exile. The Babylonians claimed their god, Marduk, was superior to the Jewish God because Marduk and the Babylonian army conquered the Jews whose God could not save them.

But Genesis 1 tells a different story. It is a defiant response and assertion to the Babylonians by a defeated and oppressed people. It is a magnificent expression of praise that proclaims that God is the Lord of life and creator of everything, not Marduk. And God saw that God's creation was good. Genesis 1 is a word of hope and encouragement to a conquered people. It gives the Jewish people their reason for why they should hold fast, believe in God, and trust in their covenantal relationship with God.

Genesis 2 is an older creation story written around 900 BCE. It is more on the lines of other ancient creation stories. Here, God is viewed anthropomorphically, as though God were like human beings, who works like a potter forming man from the dust of the earth and who walks in a garden.

Genesis 3 explains the freedom given to us by God and our misuse of it. Adam and Eve wanted to be like God so they let the serpent tempt them to eat the forbidden fruit. Do you know of any serpents who can talk? Or do we, like Adam and Eve, want the power and glory of God which leads to temptation, human disobedience, and eventually to God's discipline. Yet the story goes that God lovingly clothes Adam and Eve before their expulsion from the Garden of Eden and into their new found freedom. This gesture suggests that God offers them a new life to be lived outside of Eden.

From there, Genesis 4 introduces the concept of sin with Cain's premeditated murder of his brother Abel. I think Cain probably withheld his best from God. His jealousy and desire to be first leads to murder.

In time, people are drowning in their sins so God cleanses and recreates our world through Noah and the flood in Genesis 6.5-8.22. Please note that the Tigris and Euphrates Rivers were known to flood from time to time. We are told that God regrets this worldwide destruction of living things and decides never to use this strategy again to disciple disobedient humanity. Therefore in Genesis 9:11-17, God makes a covenant which is symbolized by the rainbow not to discipline us in this manner.

Genesis 1-11 concludes with the Tower of Babel. Men designed it to reach into the heavens so they could be like God, independent from God, and rulers of the universe. God thwarts and routs their arrogance, excessive pride, and presumptions of greatness by confusing their languages and dispersing them. Today, could this power grab be the source of wars amongst people?

Think About It

So what can we learn about God in these early Genesis' stories?

- You could say these Genesis stories recycle themselves with different characters throughout human history. Even though these stories are not history or science, they are theological statements of faith given in a story format that reflect our often broken and distorted relationship with God. Do you agree?
- Do these stories set forth our limitations and give us a moral compass? What makes you think so?
- Do you think Creator and creature are bound to each other? What makes you think so?
- Do you believe God has a purpose for us yet grants us freedom to live on our own terms?
- Why do you think the world belongs to God the Creator and not us as God's creatures?
- Do you believe God wants a loving relationship with us? What makes you think so?
- Why would God want us to be co-creators with God?
- What makes you think God wants us to be stewards, shepherds, and gardeners in our world?

I believe:

- Like a loving parent of a small child, God indulges us with our freedom and self-assertion.
- God does not abandon us and the world. Nor does God take away our free will.
- God waits patiently for us to grow up and learn that disobedience and self-centeredness have consequences.
- God uses discipline as one means for instruction.
- God gives us free will and does not coerce us into this relationship.

In these Genesis stories, our disobedience is highlighted and left unresolved and open ended.

4

WHY WORK?

L ET ME REPEAT , Genesis 1 was written during the Jewish exile in Babylonia to refute the Babylonians' belief that their gods were more powerful than the God of Israel. The Israelites would not accept this Babylonian notion even though they were living in exile under their rule. The Israelites came to the theological understanding that they deserved the punishment of exile for turning away from God and sinning. They came to believe that out of nothing God created everything. No one but God can create something out of nothing. Their response to the Babylonians is that the Israelite God is Lord and Creator of all life and their job is to be good stewards of this world and our environment.

One of my professors, William Muehl, tells us a story in his book *Why Preach? Why Listen?* about an old and traditional Jewish story that goes something like this.

"When Adam and Eve were expelled from Eden, they wasted no time in blaming each other, thus establishing the pattern for married life through the ages. For a time they considered trying to sneak back into Eden. But the gate looked forbidding and the angel with the flaming sword appeared incorruptible. So, with many a backward glance, the man and woman began their journey over the face of the earth, looking for a place to dwell.

"Some lands were too hot, others too cold. This place was a desert, that one a swamp. A few looked and felt just right proved to be shared by large man-eating animals whose urgent appetites threatened life and limb. The long days of searching dragged painfully into years.

"At last Adam and Eve came to a large fertile valley. Sweet grasses grew abundantly in it, and a clear fresh stream ran through it. Gentle, plant-eating animals grazed quietly. And fish filled the streams. Far up in one of the valley walls there was a clean, dry cave, with an apron that caught the first rays of the dawn. Here the man and woman settled down.

"Things went well for them. Adam tilled the ground and hunted for game. Eve prepared the food, sewed clothing, and grew great with child. Oh, it wasn't Eden. The night a skunk got into the butter crock Eve wept and remembered the garden. The day his plow broke on a large rock Adam cursed and reminded his wife about the apple.

"But then one night in spring, when the air was soft and fragrant with the scent of new growth, Adam lay on the apron of the cave, unable to sleep. The sky above him was splashed with stars, the muted lowing of the herds came faintly from the pastures below. Every muscle in his body ached from the labors of the day.

"Suddenly, Adam turned to his wife.

"Eve, God was wrong! This is what we're meant for. To till the ground and raise our grain. To hunt and fish for meat, to work all day in the hot sun and feel the sweat drying on our bodies in the cool of the evening. To try something and fail and try it again and fail. And keep on trying until it works. To struggle to understand things that fill us with fear. To feel hunger and thirst and pain—and hope. This is better than Eden. This is what we were meant for. God was wrong, Eve. God was wrong!

"And the story ends, somewhere so far away that the human mind cannot even imagine the distance and so near that the breath of Adam's speaking was hot against his hand. God heard the words of defiance flung by the man into the deep well of space. And hearing, God smiled."

Perhaps God smiled because God wanted humanity to discover that work is good for us and that it provides a rhythm and purpose for our lives.

As a child I use to mimic my mother's household chores. Soon enough I learned how to do them. I did not mind. These chores were a part of my daily routine of living in my parents' household. We each had our chores. And the sooner they were completed, the sooner we were free to play or do our homework.

Physical labor shows you where you have been and what you have accomplished. Working in an office or doing ministry does not show you so obviously what you have done. Yet I derive a great deal of personal satisfaction knowing that maybe, as God's servant, I may have made a difference in someone's life, especially if that difference means a person's spiritual life has been opened up and possibly enriched. To me, the life of the spirit is far more important than any material thing or comfort.

The Sabbath day has always been an important day for me. Before I became a minister, it was a day of rest, a day for worship, celebration, and remembrance. We are told in Genesis 2:2-3 that the Sabbath is the day God took a rest from his work of creation. By this action, God asserts that life does not depend upon our feverish activity of self-securing, but there can be a pause in which life is given to us simply as a gift.

Ideally, work brings meaning to life. It should give a person a sense of self-worth and of identity. But what about those who feel alienated from their work? Some may view their assembly-line, office, or trade positions as tedious. Some may have sought high-income positions, not because they like them, but rather because of the large paycheck they earn.

Unfortunately, alienated workers feel put upon by their employers. Sometimes they resent their families who depend on their earning capacity. Alienated workers have all sorts of excuses for not working and have difficulty motivating themselves to work. For them, there is no value and meaning to their work other than their paycheck. They are not proud of their work accomplishments. Work is viewed as one of the burdens of life that need to be borne rather than one of the gifts God has given us to give our lives meaning and purpose. The end result is dissatisfaction with one's life. They cannot say as God did after each act of creation: "And God saw that it was good."

Nor does feverish activity with our leisure time and extra money bring us happiness. Rabbi Harold Kushner in his book *When All You've Ever Wanted Isn't Enough* says:

> You don't become happy by pursuing happiness. You become happy by living a life that means something. The happiest people you know are probably not the richest or most famous, probably not the ones who work hardest at being happy by reading the articles and buying the books and latching on to the latest fads. I suspect that the happiest people you know are the ones who work at being kind, helpful, and reliable; and happiness sneaks into their lives while they are busy doing those things.

God is a mystery to us. And there is a mystery to our lives which God wants us to unravel and discover in our lifetime. Part of our nature and mystery is that we become bored when nothing new or different happens in our lives. Perhaps that is why we have the story of the temptation of Adam and Eve. They became bored with their idyllic existence. Where was the challenge to life? Their boredom drew them to distraction. It caused them to listen to another voice other than God's. Or was it some inner prompting urging them on or some new challenge they sought?

Perhaps God knew this would happen to them and that is why He placed in this garden the tree of knowledge, the tree of good and evil. God knew that it would be just a matter of time before Adam and Eve would become so bored with the sameness of each day that eventually they would violate His command and eat of the fruit of the tree of knowledge.

For some reason, God has given us humans the gift of ambiguity. We have to make choices in our lives with no certainty as to the result of our choices when we make them. We are defined by our choices—our educational, vocational, religious, moral, and marital choices. These choices determine who we are.

We cannot be like God. God is limitless, and we are limited. Yet there are some in this world who try to play God and assume a lofty god-like rule over others such as dictators, ayatollahs, presidents, Islamic terrorists, cults, some religious leaders, etc. These tin gods cannot conquer God and the natural order of God's world. They also have a limited life span.

Human arrogance may know no limits, but God's world provides limits. We need to acknowledge our ignorance of many of God's ways and be grateful for those revelations that God has made known to us through scripture and Jesus Christ.

Think About It

- Do you believe God created our world and why?
- Are we meant to work for our daily bread? What makes you think so?
- Where do you find your happiness?
- Do you agree with the Adam and Eve story written during the Babylonian exile? Why?
- What truths about life and God have you learned from the Genesis stories?

5

CHOICES

MY HUSBAND once told me of an incident during an air raid in World War II in Riga, Latvia, that he would never forget. He was about ten-years old at the time. The air raid sirens were blasting. Everyone ran to the nearest air-raid shelter. A woman in her fifties was racing to the shelter in which my husband was. But she could not run as fast as other people because she was loaded down with two suitcases that slowed her movements. The people in the shelter yelled to her to drop her suitcases and to run for cover. She refused to let go of those two suitcases and was killed.

After the air raid, the men in the shelter went to pick her up and to put her on the death wagon. They looked through her suitcases and found nothing of value. Perhaps the contents totaled $50. From that time forward, my husband believed that the only worthwhile possessions a person can have is his or her education, training, and relationship with God. These possessions weigh nothing and can go wherever the fortunes of life will lead someone.

This woman was not free from the tyranny of things. I wonder whether she owned the possessions or did the possessions own her. I wonder what her idolatries were and her relationship to God.

Christians are oriented in faith towards the incarnation, teachings, death, and resurrection of Jesus Christ. Christians make a free decision and commitment to live as best they can a Christ-like life of faith and obedience to God. This approach to life sounds simple, but it really is not. The apostle Paul describes his struggle with sin (Romans 7:14-25) which wants to dominate his life. Paul, as a Pharisee, tried to live by an infallible list of things which ought to and ought not to be done. After his conversion, Paul learned that the Law was spiritual and from God. It was people that twisted and distorted the Law God had given Moses.

The purpose of the Law was to lead God's people to a new and better life with God. But people were keeping the rules for all the wrong reasons. They were keeping them not out of a pure and grateful love of God. They were keeping the rules with a view to winning rewards for themselves. They felt that their good deeds would require God to shower God's favor on them. They did not understand that God cannot be bought or forced into giving them what they want. Yet a lot of people today will disagree with me. They accept without questioning today's prosperity gospel promoted by Joel Osteen and others.

Paul learned that Christ came to show us a new way to live and die. It is this New Covenant or life in Christ that sets people free from their sin and wrong intentions. The New Covenant asks us to look at ourselves and our relationship with God in terms of love and refraining from doing harm to ourselves and our neighbors. Paul understood that while there is much that is willful about sin, there is also much that seems to be the result of our having yielded our control or allegiance to another spirit, being, or thing which takes control over us and from which we cannot free ourselves.

God gives us freedom. So, what is freedom? We could say that it is the absence of constraints. One theologian said

"Freedom is an open space not yet filled up." I like that definition, Freedom is an open space not yet filled up. It is a piece of unfinished creation in which we can shape our humanity and our environment. We are unfinished beings. We are capable of moving into possibilities that have still to be unfolded. However, this freedom involves risk for both God and ourselves. Since God gives us freedom, we can either cooperate with God for good or disassociate ourselves from God by freely giving our allegiance to an evil cause or in selfish pursuits.

For example, our relationship to God may be similar to that of the prodigal son and his father (Luke 15:11-32). Let us say that the father represents God. The prodigal son represents those who do not wish to live according to God's wishes. The elder brother represents those who try to win merit from God through their observance of the Law.

The father loves both sons. Both sons represent possible ways of living, neither way being correct. The prodigal son through wanton living fills up his open space with harmful desires and deeds. He does not do God's work. He becomes spiritually bankrupt. When he wakes up and realizes his condition, he repents, returns home, and will be glad to be a servant in his father's home. His father accepts him because the prodigal son realizes what wrong he has done and repents of it. It took real courage, a setting aside of his pride, and true repentance for him to return home. And it took forgiveness on the father's part to accept the repentant prodigal and restore a relationship with him.

The elder son is self-righteous and believes he has earned his preferred standing with his father. The elder son's freedom or open space ties into other people's open space. That space should have been filled with love for God and others. Instead the elder son's lack of love for his brother causes him to want to exclude his brother from occupying any open space. Nor did the elder son wish his father to look favorably upon his prodigal brother and give him some open space.

We could say that the freedom Christ gives us is more difficult to exercise. We are to love God, one another, and refrain
from harming others. What the elder son fails to realize is that
God loves us all, that we all stand bankrupt like the prodigal son
before God. We cannot earn a preferred standing before God. It is
God's love for us and His gift of grace towards us that enable us
to stand before God.

In the New Covenant (Luke 22:20), we are not forced to love
God. If we were, we would have no freedom. God gives us our
freedom. God waits like the prodigal son's father did with open,
loving arms. In making a commitment to God, people are relating
to God by entrusting their entire future and way of life to God
and the possibilities which that way of life may offer them.

But keep in mind that Christians do not live enchanted lives.
We have no special protection. That is the price of our freedom.
We must struggle between our harmful desires and the New
Covenant way of life. The same amount of rain and life's problems occur in our lives as in the lives of non-Christians. The
difference is that Christians, with God's help, should be able to
cope or deal better with life's problems than non-Christians. True
freedom is internal.

We know from nature that a void is never allowed to remain
unfilled. What occupies that space are the choices we make. We
can fill our open space with busyness, running from one meeting
or activity to another. Or we can fill it with drinking, drug use,
sexual escapades, excessive acquisition of material wealth and
power, unbelief, idolatries, and/or violence. Many people try to
find meaning and authenticity for their lives apart from God
through such activities. Others accept the grace of God, fill freedom's open space with love and trust in God, respect God and
God's creation, live a Christian life, and are part of a Christian
community.

Are we free? Yes, we are within certain limitations. Our
freedom is directed by our inner conscience. Our conscience

presupposes the exercise of rational judgment, or discrimination between truth and error, and of the moral life. We find true freedom and autonomy by not giving our total or complete allegiance to material things or other beings.

Instead we can live in complete obedience and dependence on God and thereby find true freedom. Perhaps our greatest freedom occurs when we think beyond ourselves and lose our concern for ourselves and have concern for others. That is why Jesus said: "Whoever would save his life shall lose it; and whoever loses his life for my sake…will save it." (Matthew 16:24-26)

Think About It

- How would you describe freedom?
- Do you believe we are able to find true freedom in God's service? What makes you think so?
- Why or why not do you believe your good deeds require God to shower God's favor on you?
- Why does Jesus cast the elder brother in the prodigal son parable as being self-righteous?
- Do you know people like the elder brother? What similarities do they share?

6

ENDINGS

THE STORY of Joseph found in the Old Testament (Genesis 37+) is a story of family conflict fueled by favoritism. It is not a pretty story. No one is in the right. Jacob, the father, prefers Joseph over his other sons. This overindulgent love causes Jacob to give Joseph a regal robe with long sleeves which Joseph proudly and arrogantly wears in front of everyone.

In Joseph's day, workers wore sleeveless tunics. Joseph's long-flowing robe publicly displays Joseph's preferred status. Joseph's brothers despise this robe and all that it represents. They feel they are unloved by their father. Yet they need and want to be loved by him. They are just as worthy as Joseph if not more so since they are the elder brothers who do most of the work.

Joseph is loved too much by Jacob and is overindulged. Joseph encourages favoritism and reinforces it by carrying false reports to his father about his brothers. Jacob believes these reports. Love and preference blind Jacob to the consequences of his actions. So, in a sense Joseph's bad reports exist in the fantasy world of Jacob and Joseph and are not subjected to a reality check. This purposeful delusion is impossible for Joseph's brothers to counter and correct. The brothers are found guilty without a fair trial. They feel helpless.

When Joseph begins to have dreams, he tells everyone his dreams because they enhance his position. Dreams were believed to be channels of divine communication. The wise interpreter of dreams could discern the course of the future. Joseph's dreams show him as being the recipient of God's divine favor and being the bearer and fulfillment of God's promises to Abraham.

The dream regarding the sheaves of grain symbolically points forward both to Joseph's management of Egypt's grain supplies and to the future grain-buying expeditions of his starving brothers. When that occurs, the brothers will assume the posture of obeisance and servitude. In fact, their very survival will depend upon Joseph.

The second dream regarding the sun, the moon, and the 11 stars includes the prostration of Joseph's parents as well as his brothers. Each dream alludes to Joseph's superior position over his brothers and his parents. These dreams are too much for Joseph's brothers to bear. Even Jacob rebukes Joseph. Joseph has gone too far. His brothers' hate increases. They decide to take action before things get any worse for themselves. They will wait for the right opportunity to come along.

The day finally comes when Jacob sends Joseph to check on his brothers who are roaming the countryside with their flocks. At first, Joseph cannot find them. Symbolically, he is lost. He is suspended between two worlds—that of his loving father behind him and the world of his hate-filled brothers ahead of him.

Joseph's brothers, in the meantime, have situated themselves and their flocks so that they can see and prepare themselves for any people or wild animals that may come upon them and bring potential danger to them and their flocks. When they see Joseph approaching, they have sufficient time to plot against Joseph. They take Joseph prisoner. All brothers except for Reuben and Judah wish to kill Joseph. Reuben and Judah believe that blood cannot be spilled and concealed. Spilled blood calls for vengeance. Rueben and Judah have their scheme for saving Joseph. But neither scheme works.

Joseph is stripped of his beautiful robe and thrown into a waterless and dark cistern with no water or light. The brothers all want to stop the future from occurring. They want to dethrone Joseph. A symbolic death occurs. Midianite merchants draw Joseph from the pit and sell him to Ishmaelites going to Egypt.

Back home, Jacob becomes inconsolable when he is given Joseph's bloodied robe. His grief causes him to feel empty, bitter, and skeptical of life. All hope is gone. He does not want to go on. He believes God's promises to Abraham have died with Joseph. Jacob rejects any intimacy with his living children. Jacob's family unity is destroyed by favoritism, hostility, hatred, treachery, and deception.

An end of one way of life has occurred. Life will never be the same again. But the author of the Joseph story does not say the story is ended. The dream does not depend on the father and Joseph's brothers. The dream stands on its own. The author suggests that God's hidden plan prevails over human plans. Yes, Joseph will never see Canaan again. He is sold as a slave to Potiphar, the captain of Pharaoh's guard. Joseph will have to give up his present identity and social conditioning if he is to survive. No longer will he enjoy a favored status. He will need to let go of the past and not be a prisoner of it.

Joseph's story is our story. Our lives are not one continuous round of sameness regarding our relationships to each other and to God. Things happen to us. Every significant transition in life begins with an ending. We have to let go of the old before we can pick up the new—and not just outwardly. Inwardly we need to let go of connections to those people and places that have acted as definition of whom we are, be it husband, wife, mother, student, daughter, son, minister, boss, job, and retiree.

Letting go is hard to do. Often it requires a change in defined roles and relationships. At best, letting go is an ambiguous experience. For Joseph, it was sudden and abrupt. Endings can be gradual and/or abrupt.

Letting go involves developing new skills for negotiating the perilous passage across the 'nowhere' that separates the old life situation from the new. But before that can be done, we need to understand our own characteristic ways of coping with endings.

Endings are the first phase of transition before a new beginning occurs. Between the ending and the new beginning, there is an empty, fallow time in between. Old connections are severed. If we are frightened and insecure, we are likely to abort the necessary three-phase process of ending, transition, and new beginning. If we are in a hurry to get through the transitional time, we will deny ourselves the opportunity for healing that enables us to make a new beginning.

Think About It

- If you were one of Joseph's brothers, how would you break the cycle of favoritism they experienced?
- Can anyone justify favoritism among their children? What makes you think so?
- Would you say that Jacob was an abusive parent? What makes you think so?
- Do you know families like Jacob's? What makes them dysfunctional?
- What are your thoughts on sibling rivalry?

7

THE NEUTRAL ZONE

JOSEPH'S FREEDOM IS GONE. How will he survive? What feelings do you suppose he had? He is cut off from his roots. Blaming someone else or carrying false tales will not help. All his past modus operandi will no longer work. No one is concerned about his welfare. No one shows him any compassion. His outrage, sense of betrayal, bitterness, and hostility can be vented against no one but himself.

Joseph can do one of two things. He can hang onto negative feelings and let them destroy him. Or he can give them up. At this point, the scripture is silent about Joseph's mental state. We can assume he gave up negative thoughts because his stature, youth, intelligence, disposition and resourcefulness must have been sufficiently good for Potiphar to buy him. Potiphar entrusts Joseph with everything. Potiphar recognizes that blessings have flowed to him and that he has prospered since Joseph entered his household. Potiphar did not know that Joseph carried the blessing promised to Abraham.

The Joseph we meet in Egypt is much different from the Joseph we met in Canaan. Joseph's rude awakening from his fantasy world changed him. He must have taken a long hard look at himself, examined the consequences of his past behavior, and resolved never to endanger his life again by disobeying God's moral law.

The Joseph we now meet is morally upright and will not take advantage of his position and the freedom given him. He is not arrogant and proud. And he will not accept the blunt invitation by Potiphar's wife to sleep with her. Joseph speaks of Potiphar's trust in him and refuses to break his master's trust and to sin against God's moral order. When Joseph continues to rebuff her advances, Potiphar's wife abruptly replaces words with action. Failing to seduce Joseph, she vindictively charges Joseph with attempted rape.

Potiphar's wife represents Egypt and those places and people that corrupt people by seducing them into their way of thinking, doing, and living. The ones who have money or power tend to think they are beyond the reach of God's moral law or even good common sense. You could say that modern-day seducers range from drugs, alcohol, sex, gambling casinos, lotteries, human traffickers, despots, ayatollahs, presidents, gang and mob leaders, slavery, etc. Self-seeking and hedonistic pleasure seeking are characteristic of these people.

Joseph recognizes this attitude and behavior as a sure way to self-destruction. His earlier self-seeking behavior with his brothers taught him a life-changing lesson. This time, a new Joseph, a reformed Joseph, stands for integrity and moral good and not self-seeking. He will not take advantage of his position or the trust vested in him.

Strangely enough, Potiphar must have known Joseph's innocence because he did not exact the prescribed punishment of execution for such a crime. Instead Potiphar has Joseph thrown into Pharaoh's privileged prison.

Joseph finds favor with the jailer and meets Pharaoh's butler and baker there whose dreams he interprets.

A few years later when nobody can interpret Pharaoh's

dream, the chief butler recalls Joseph's ability to interpret dreams. Pharaoh orders Joseph to appear before him.

The summoning of Joseph to appear before Pharaoh to interpret his dreams is Joseph's first step towards freedom. Joseph's entrance is dramatic. A wise and mature Joseph emerges from Pharaoh's prison at age 33. He has been either a slave or a prisoner for 13 years. Now he neither acts like a slave or a prisoner nor has he a slave's mentality or mannerisms. Instead he is now shaped by the vision given to him by God.

Evil doers, slavery, and imprisonment cannot undo this vision. Joseph knows he can interpret Pharaoh's dreams because the Spirit of God is with him. No longer does Joseph take the praise and glory for his gifts. He gives God all the credit and all the glory.

Not only can Joseph interpret Pharaoh's two dreams and tell Pharaoh that the seven years of plenty and seven years of famine are fixed by God, but Joseph also has a practical plan. He does not believe that Pharaoh should sit around and wring his hands at the bad news but should take positive action to take his nation through the predicted famine. Pharaoh acknowledges God working through Joseph, accepts the validity of Joseph's interpretation of his dreams, and appoints Joseph governor over all of Egypt, second only in power to himself.

Joseph has learned to face the realities of life. He has traumatically and successfully passed through the disintegration of self-identity. He was forced to pass through the empty space between one life phase and the next. He had to die to one form of existence and identity to achieve a newer, richer life. During this transitional time, a new sense of self and integrity emerged. He entered into a new reality caused by his suffering and discontinuity with his past. He has a deepened sense of identity and purpose. He knows he is and will continue to be the bearer of the promise and blessing made to Abraham.

Joseph's story tells us many things. We learn that we may

have to endure years of separation, death, humility, false accusations, and economic or physical slavery before relief comes. During these difficult times, we need to hang on to hope. We are to live life at great risk. It must be lived in the face of deceit, temptation, and seduction on the one hand and a steadfast belief in God's presence in our lives which leads and guides us on the other hand. As God showed loyalty to Joseph, so also will God show loyalty to God's own today. God does not accept the verdict nor the power of a Potiphar's wife and today's pleasure and power seekers.

Joseph struggled with real life issues and real faith issues. He lived in the real world and learned how to be faithful to God at the same time. He did not compartmentalize his life. He felt and knew God's presence in everything he did. He was a practical man inspired to greatness by the vision given to him by God. We all can possess that inspiration and vision if we allow God to be a part of our lives.

We learn from Joseph that we cannot stop the future from occurring. His life's story tells us that sometimes in order to get from place A to place B, we need to go into a neutral zone or place of transition while we endure hardship, grow up, mature, rethink who we are, become wiser, purer, and more focused.

Think About It

- How impatient are you for a better future to open up for you?
- Why or why not would you lose hope during a transitional time in your life?
- What lessons can you learn from Joseph's life?

8

A FAMILY AFFAIR

JOSEPH'S DREAMS begin to be fulfilled. He is in charge of Egypt's food supply and now has the power of life and death over all those seeking food. Refugees stream into Egypt in search of food. Joseph's brothers are among them.

After 13 years, the brothers who tried to destroy him and the dream from occurring come begging for food. Joseph's actions towards them seem cruel. Learn more by reading Genesis 42:1-38. He accuses them of being spies and hides his identity by using an interpreter to speak to them in their own language. Joseph learns that his father and younger brother are still alive.

Jacob is still firmly in charge. Favoritism still dominates. Jacob's behavior is dysfunctional. He still mourns the presumed death of Joseph. Jacob's grief has power over them. They are all living in a mental prison. Jacob orders them around as though they were little children. He seems to have no feelings towards any of them or their children. The only person he seems capable of loving is Benjamin, the son of his beloved Rachel. Jacob keeps Benjamin a virtual prisoner for fear harm may come to him. In one way or another, Jacob harms all his family. Why?

Perhaps the answer is generational. If we look back at Jacob's life, we find he is the second born son of Isaac and Rebecca. He is the twin brother of Esau from whom he stole his birthright. With the help of Jacob's mother, he steals from Esau his father's dying blessing. Jacob's parents each had their favorite son. Isaac favored Esau and Rebecca favored Jacob. This favoritism brought dissension, hate, and eventual geographic and emotional separation between these brothers.

When Esau learned of Jacob's theft, Esau threatens to kill Jacob upon the death of their father. With only the clothes on his back, Jacob runs for his life. His and his mother's scheming and treachery rewarded him with nothing.

Jacob seeks refuge with his uncle Laban in Haran. He falls in love with Rachel, one of Laban's daughters. Since Jacob has no money, he agrees to work for seven years in exchange for Rachel's hand in marriage. Wedding day comes. The bride is heavily veiled. The marriage celebrations last into the night. The next morning Jacob awakens and finds that he is married to Rachel's sister, Leah, and not to Rachel.

Jacob has met his match in Laban who will continue to use Jacob to his advantage. Laban will agree to let Jacob marry Rachel at the end of the week if Jacob will agree to work another seven years. Jacob agrees. Love between sisters is replaced by competition for Jacob's attention and affection. Leah bears ten sons for Jacob. Rachel has difficulty conceiving any. Yet Leah remains unloved and rejected by Jacob. Eventually Rachel gives birth to Joseph. Many years later, Benjamin is born; but Rachel dies in childbirth.

Jacob was tricked into a marriage he did not want. There was no emotional commitment on his part. Leah did what her father told her to do. Perhaps she could have resisted her father, but the consequences would have been severe. The children of Jacob's and Leah's marriage were unloved by Jacob. Their sole function seemed to be a form of menial servitude.

Because Jacob loved Rachel, he loved and preferred their son

Joseph. Jacob's love was a suffocating love that almost destroyed Joseph. It was Joseph's good fortune to be separated from Jacob, to be made to endure hardship on his own, and then to achieve release from that hardship. We learn that suffocating love and over protection of our children can cause stunted emotional, spiritual, and psychological growth. Unwittingly, our over protection of children often prevents them from learning how to stand on their own two feet.

Jacob's aberrations stem from his upbringing and the win/lose psychology of deceit. Joseph's brothers seem to be an undifferentiated group that is bound by the same mother and a common crime against Joseph.

Biblical scholar Walter Brueggemann suggests "The brothers have no room to act, no energy for imagination, and no possibility of freedom. They are bound by the power of an unforgiven past, immobilized by guilt, and driven by anxiety... As a result, they are excessively concerned for the safety and well-being of their father and Benjamin."

Having once grieved their father over Joseph, they are on their guard not to grieve him further. They fail to see themselves as the bearers of the promise—the future twelve tribes of Israel. They are incapable of thinking beyond the present. They lack faith in God and God's promises. And consequently, they have no hope.

Famine and starvation threaten Jacob and his family. Jacob sends his sons to Egypt with little care for their well-being with these words. "I have heard that there is grain in Egypt; go down and buy grain for us there, that we may live, and not die." His lingering grief for Joseph and his anticipated grief for Benjamin should any harm come to him cause Jacob to keep Benjamin at home.

Think About It

- Do you know families like Jacob's?
- Today, is a parent justified in preferring one child over another? What makes you think so?
- What causes child abuse mentally, physically, emotionally, and psychologically?
- From the scripture reading of Genesis 42:1-38, what do you think of Joseph's behavior toward his brothers?

9

FORGIVENESS AND RECONCILIATION

I DO NOT WANT to repeat here the intriguing Genesis stories about Joseph and Jacob that are so well written in Genesis 37-50. Please take the time to read them. What follows below is my attempt to give you my thoughts on these scriptural passages.

Joseph does not let his brothers know who he is. His peculiar treatment of his brothers makes us think he has revenge on his mind. Joseph had been grievously wronged by them and suffered much because of them. Why shouldn't he seek revenge? He has the perfect opportunity to exact any kind of revenge he wants. Why did Joseph behave the way he did?

Joseph may have gone through a stage of anger, hurt, and thoughts of revenge. But early on in Egypt, Joseph must have let go and brought to an end all those feelings, because God was with him. Joseph could not be open to the healing power of God if he continued to harbor negative, destructive thoughts. Such negative thoughts would have dictated his moral behavior and would have stood in the way of any healthy relationships and his moral and psychological health.

Though he were a slave and prisoner, he refused to allow himself to be held in bondage by his hatreds. Therefore, at some point Joseph forgave his brothers of their sin against him. Joseph's forgiveness saved him and allowed him to grow spiritually and psychologically.

Similarly, many of us may have been wronged by others. Some of us are incapable of forgiveness and getting on with our lives. Instead, we nurture our wounds and let them grow like a cancer within us. We feel a certain power and moral superiority toward our offenders. We think they are the low lifers, and we will not let them forget it. In a sense, we may enjoy our martyrdom. The more we enjoy it, the more our identity and self-image become fueled by the wrongs once done to us. Vengeance and hatred gnaw away at our once healthy minds.

Many people think Joseph's strange behavior with his brothers suggest a cruel form of revenge. I do not agree with them. I believe he acts the way he does to test his brothers' moral health. When he had last been with them, they were so concerned with themselves and jealous of him that they were prepared to kill him. Joseph wanted to know whether they were the same now as they were then. His testing of them through the entrapment and possible death of Benjamin tells Joseph all he wants to know. He learns that his brothers feel guilty about their treatment of him. They believe their present ill fortune is a result of their sin of long ago. Not only had they had to live with that sin on their souls all these years, but they had to maintain the lie and silence about Joseph.

Joseph knew through his own forgiveness of them, that to make a new beginning between himself and his brothers, there needed to be a change in his brothers' moral character. The slate between them had to be wiped clean. Had they learned through their father's suffering that he and others were more important to their lives than their own self-centered needs and desires?

Judah was ready to offer his life as a substitute for Benjamin so that their father will live. Judah pleads: "How can I go back to my father if the boy is not with me? I cannot bear to see this disaster come upon my father."

On hearing Judah's plea, Joseph is overwhelmed with emotion and joy to hear that his brothers had truly repented of their sin against him and would never dream of committing another similar sin against their father by allowing harm to come to Benjamin. The brothers have grown morally. They no longer concern themselves with favoritism, birthrights, inheritance, or position in the tribe. They love and care for each other and especially their father. Joseph now knows that all obstacles are removed for a new beginning between them to occur. They had truly repented of their sin against Joseph. They are not the same men they were years ago.

When Joseph tells them who he is, they stand in dismay before him. They do not know that Joseph long ago had forgiven them. They fear reprisal. But Joseph says that God had providentially ordered his fate for the sake of preserving their family with food. This interpretation by Joseph of their experiences delivers his brothers from fear of revenge and from mutual recrimination. His brothers are not absolved of their crime, but their crime can now be accepted in the light of God's overarching, all-inclusive providence.

Many of us can take Joseph's explanation for all the ill that befell him as God's will. Personally, I have difficulty with such an interpretation. I do not believe that the tragedies we experience are because God wills them. How can we say that God is responsible for natural disasters, moral evil, and/or the death of a child? These thoughts may give some people comfort, but they do not comfort me. I do not believe God is the author of evil. God did not interfere with those evil people who crucified Jesus. God did not interfere with the Holocaust. Evil exists because people fail to stand up against it.

Unfortunately, circumstances may turn many people against God. And in their anger, accuse God of inflicting evil and pain upon them and their loved ones. Often we seek answers for the unfortunate things that happen to us when, in fact, there may be no answer. Or we may already know the answer but do not want to accept it.

If our faith is to survive, we need to discover a way to come to terms with the unfairness and the afflictions of life. Let me suggest that the act of forgiving the offender and, yes, forgiving God, if we believe God is the offender, releases the poison, the bitterness, and the resentment for the wrongs done us. Similar to Joseph, this release will allow us to make a fresh start and live a new life.

Think About It

- What have you done or could you do about someone who has threatened the trajectory of your life?
- Are you able to forgive and let go the great evil that has impacted your life? How so?
- Should a rapist and/or human trafficker be forgiven or should they be judged in a court of law and be sentenced to prison?
- Do you believe that evil exists because people fail to challenge and stop it?

10

MEETING GOD

Exodus 2:23-3:17

WITH THE APPROVAL OF PHARAOH, Joseph invites all his relatives to resettle in Egypt in the fertile land of Goshen. There they increase in number over a time period of approximately 500 years.

During Joseph's time, the Pharaohs of Egypt were not themselves Egyptians, but rather Hyksos, members of a nomadic Bedouin tribe, that invaded Egypt from the east with horses and chariots. Before the Hyksos' arrival, Egyptians had never seen horses, and the Egyptian armies were routed by the mounted nomads.

The Hyksos settled in as ruling Pharaohs. It is believed that the general Egyptian population disliked these foreign Pharaohs. It is possible that the famine crisis of Joseph's time deepened this hostility towards the Hyksos Pharaohs and perhaps toward Joseph and his family. When the Hyksos fell from power, the persecution and enslavement of the Hebrews began. Genesis 47:13-26 gives more information about this part of the story.

Around the year 1250 BCE, the enslaved Israelites are about to be rescued by Moses. Let him tell you how it all happened.

"My name is Moses. I am here today to help you answer an important question—who is God? Before meeting God, my notion of God was based mostly on stories told to me by Egyptians in Pharaoh's palace. Then after my escape from Egypt to Midian, I learned about God from Jethro, my father-in-law.

"Somehow all these stories did not make God real to me. I did not know or feel God's presence in my life. I did not know what God was like. In fact, I was angry with all gods and Jethro's God especially for allowing the Israelites to suffer under Pharaoh's relentless whip and enslavement. If God were God, why did God allow the suffering and oppression of the Israelites to continue?

"Then, one day, while tending and minding sheep, my curiosity drew me to an unusual sight. I saw a flame of fire in the midst of a bush that did not burn. As I approached the bush, a voice called out to me. 'Moses, Moses!' I answered, 'Here am I.' And the voice said to me: 'Do not come near; keep your distance; and take off your sandals from your feet, for the place on which you are standing is holy ground.'

"I looked around me and saw no one. The voice actually came from the bush. Then I realized God was making Godself known to me in something as lowly as a burning bush. God was going to enter a conversation with me. So, I took off my sandals and covered my face and waited for God to speak to me again.

"It seemed God's concern was my concern. God was concerned about my people who were suffering in Egypt with no possibility of release. My pulse quickened. Maybe, God would rescue my people. Maybe, the time had come for God to keep the promise of land, posterity, and blessings that God had made to Abraham. Maybe, Jethro's God is a God who hears, remembers, sees, and knows all. After all, God said He was the God of my Israelite father, of Abraham, of Isaac, and of Jacob. These were my thoughts. But my thoughts were only a part of God's thoughts.

"God surprised me. God asked ME to lead the Israelites out of the land of Egypt. Ridiculous! How could I solve that problem? I even asked God, 'Who am I that I should go to Pharaoh and bring the sons of Israel out of Egypt?' Had God forgotten that I was a fugitive for having killed an Egyptian overseer? Had God forgotten that I was not one of the Israelites? I was an outsider. I was raised in Pharaoh's palace. No, God I cannot go. I am of no help to You. The Israelites will laugh at me, and Pharaoh will execute me.

"Then God said: 'I will be with you. I will work in and through you in Egypt.'

"God did not seem to understand the impossibility of the task. For starters I asked God: 'Well, if you are going to be with me, whom shall I say sent me?' God's answer confused me. God said: 'I AM WHO I AM.' In essence God was saying, I will be what I will be. I will cause to be what I will cause to be as I am the Creator. I will be God for you. That is all you need to know. By telling you this much, I become accessible to you and to others. I am opening up a part of myself to you and to the Israelite leaders. That is all you need to know for now.

"God! Why would anyone believe me? I was a part of the enemy camp. They will not trust me. Remember what happened when I tried to save an Israelite from an Egyptian overseer's lashes and when I tried to break up two Israelites who were struggling with each other? They asked me: 'Who made you a prince and a judge over us?'

"So, I began to give God excuses why I was not the right person to send on this assignment. I said they would not believe me or listen to my voice because you did not appear to me. Then God said: 'Take the rod that is in your hand and cast it on the ground.' The rod turned into a live serpent. It frightened me and I fled from it. Then God ordered me to put out my hand and to take it by the tail. I did what God told me to do. The serpent became a rod again.

"Then God told me to put my hand into my bosom. When I took it out, my hand was leprous and as white as snow. God told me to put my hand back into my bosom. So, I put my hand back into my bosom. And when I took it out, it was restored like the rest of my flesh. God said, 'If they will not believe you or heed the first sign, they may believe the second sign. If they will not believe even these two signs or heed your voice, you shall take some water from the Nile and pour it upon the dry ground. And the water which you shall take from the Nile will become blood upon the dry ground.'

"End of my excuses and argument? No! I had one last chance to get out of God's rescue plan. I told God: 'I am not eloquent. I am slow of speech and tongue.' I could tell God's patience with me was running out. God said: 'Who has made man's mouth? Who makes him dumb, or deaf, or seeing, or blind? Is it not I, the Lord? Now therefore go, and I will be with your mouth and teach you what you shall speak. Nothing is impossible for those who do my will.'

"Finally, I said to God: 'Oh, my Lord, send, I pray some other person.' Then the anger of the Lord was kindled against me. God told me that Aaron, my brother, would help me in saying what needs to be said and that God would be with my mouth and will teach me what I must do.

"A new day had come. I went to Egypt to do the impossible, to take an enslaved people, and to lead them to freedom.

"That was many, many years ago. Little did I know at that time the possibilities that would open up to me and for my people. I would come to know, trust, and love God over the years. Yes, I fought with God whenever things did not go well. Sometimes I wanted out. The Israelites were a stiff necked and uncooperative people. And Pharaoh's heart was full of disbelief.

He did not believe my God was God. In fact, Pharaoh thought he was god. He had an important lesson to learn.

"Also, I argued with God. I resisted God. God listened to my problems and objections. We had a good give and take often before we reached a compromise on how to overcome a particular obstacle. Life was not easy for me even though God was with me.

"So, from Mt. Horeb, I left holy ground with a holy mission. Was I ready for it? No. How can anyone be fully ready for God's mission? What I did have going for me was my knowledge of Egyptian ways, the Egyptian court, and the Egyptian mindset because I had been reared in that environment. Perhaps God had no one else like me to send.

"The fire that was in the burning bush that day entered my heart and mind. It took hold of me and burned. It gave me a faith in God even though I did not fully know God. Yet I decided to trust in God. From the burning bush onward, God showed me many things about Godself.

"I am only one of a cloud of witnesses to our great God. But one thing I do know, our God identifies with the hungry, the displaced, the suffering, and the oppressed. Our God suffers with them. Yet God has great self-restraint. God will not overpower the oppressors. We, who are God's servants must do that job. God will only work through other people who are willing to risk doing great things for God and God's people. I learned that God wanted to create a new society— one away from the seductions of Egypt. So, God helped the Israelites and me to leave Egypt. God did not force us to leave. We had to take the first step in faith and trust and then another and another step."

Think About It

- Do you believe Moses' story?

- Why do you think the burning bush was not consumed?
- How does God come to different people?
- What excuses do people give for not doing God's will?
- Why do the Jewish people think Moses is the most important person of their faith ancestors?
- With God's help, what can people accomplish? Why do or don't people do God's will?

11

EXCUSES, EXCUSES

EXCUSES. We all make them. Children often use excuses to shift blame away from themselves. Adults make choices and give themselves an excuse to explain whatever action or lack of action they decide to take. Often excuses stand in the shadow of a dilemma. Is an excuse the twin sister of a quandary? Can a thorny problem be avoided by an excuse?

What can we learn from Moses' excuses and their religious significance?

The first religious significance is that the Israelites interpreted their trials as well as those of the Egyptians as a contest between God and Pharaoh. Pharaoh represents the rulers of the world. These rulers are political, economic, and spiritual rulers who hold the line against all threatened opposition to their power. They can and do sacrifice peoples' well-being and lives to stay in power.

The Israelites, on the other hand, also had to recognize the fact that their God who freed them was a God who demanded a response of trust, worship, and obedience from them. They came to realize that God is not an indifferent God and that God is a jealous God and will not let them worship other gods without serious consequences.

I don't think God's expectations for us have changed much over the centuries. This story of the struggle with Pharaoh becomes today's paradigm for understanding the divine-human relationship of bondage and freedom, of excuse and rationalization, of belief and disbelief.

Today, heads of state, military officers, judges, corporate leaders, bankers, religious leaders, police, and so on, too often play the role of Pharaoh. They THINK or ACT as though they are ABOVE the law. They decide who wins and who loses, who lives and who dies, who will succeed and who will fail.

The second religious significance of the Exodus story is that God wants us to renounce idolatrous society and beliefs. God wants to set us apart so that we can be shaped into a faith community devoted to God alone. For such a new society to begin, the Israelites had to have a complete break from their past for a new order to occur. And thus, we have their wilderness experience. In the wilderness, Moses forges a new social order with equalitarian laws and justice all mediated through the faith community.

We do not think of ourselves as an idolatrous society bowing down and doing obeisance to some lifeless statue. But do we trust in an unseen and unknowable God or do we only trust in that which we can see, touch, and hear with our own senses?

In 1933, Dietrich Bonhoeffer, in a radio broadcast urged the German people not to turn Hitler into an idol. He feared "the image of the leader will gradually become the image of the 'misleader'.... This is the leader who makes an idol of himself and his office, and who thus mocks God."

The third religious significance of the Exodus texts is that Moses, inspired by God, no longer lacks determination, confidence, a vocation, and a mission and purpose in life. He no longer runs from responsibility and leadership. Moses knows God is with him and will give him the necessary strength and vision for nation building. Through doing God's work, Moses is freed from all that held him in bondage. He becomes the central person in the Old Testament.

Once the Israelites escape from Egypt, trouble and rebellion brew in the camp. The freed Israelites lack unity and a common vision. They do not know how to take responsibility for their lives. They do not place their trust in God or in Moses. The security, no matter how harsh as a slave, for many was better than the insecurity of wilderness life. Many Israelites cannot accept freedom with its accompanying uncertainty. They wish to return to their former lives of slavery and certainty in Egypt.

People experience a sense of loss when they make a break from their past, a break from the status quo. It takes a lot of mental, emotional, physical, and spiritual strength and courage to let go of what holds us in bondage.

In life, we meet with a call to duty, some voluntary, some forced by law and unavoidable. It is the voluntary duty that presents to us the difficult choice to serve God or not to serve God. It is the same choice Moses had to make. Moses' call and response is a metaphor for spiritual growth and what can happen to a person when he or she is dedicated to God's call be the job great or small.

The story of the Israelites' slavery repeats itself today. Who are today's pharaohs (tyrants) who oppress the voiceless and powerless minorities many of whom tough it out in their home country rather than venture into an unknown and uncertain future? Who among these pharaohs have a hardened heart? A few good examples to think about are:

- The genocide of the Rohingya Muslims of Myanmar. Many of the survivors escaped to Bangladesh and live in refugee camps. Reporters of the Buddhist army's crimes against the Rohingyas have been jailed. And Nobel Peace Prize winner Aung Sun Suu Kyi did nothing to help the Rohingya.

- African and Middle East refugees running from violence in their home countries put their lives at risk trying to reach Europe by land and sea, many of whom are denied entry and/or die at sea.
- Millions of Uighur Muslims in China are put into concentration and re-education camps. Children are separated from parents. Women are sterilized. And those not imprisoned are under surveillance.
- Russian journalists and opposition leaders are beaten, clubbed, imprisoned, poisoned, and/or shot if they fail to promote idolization of Putin in the news.
- United States citizens, news reporters, U.S. Senators and Representatives are vilified by Donald Trump if they fail to agree publicly with him and his authoritarian dictates.

Might doesn't make right.

- Make your list of today's pharaohs.
- And then ask yourself; How does your self-interest determine your loyalty?
- Do you have a hardened heart?
- Are today's pharaohs your god?
- Should they be?
- What about the God of the Israelites and Christians and God's demands on you?

When I feel helpless against today's pharaohs and their machinations, I remind myself what Isaiah says about God.

Those who wait for the Lord shall renew their strength, they shall mount up with wings like eagles, they shall run and not be weary, and they shall walk and not faint. (Isaiah 40:31)

We, too, can be like Moses should God call us to do a job. We, too, can succeed against overwhelming odds if we develop a trusting, selfless working relationship with God. As long as God is with us, no one, no event can defeat us mentally or spiritually. That does not mean that we will not have our moments of depression, discouragement, and physical defeat. But we will learn from these experiences what we should or should not have done and be able to move forward on our God-given mission.

Life and the decisions we have to make are not simple. We cannot cut ourselves off from the dominant culture like the Israelites in the wilderness did. We can live within our culture but with an alternative vision given to us through the Bible. As God's people, we can help the oppressed and the needy. Like Moses, ask God the hard questions. The answers may come in an unexpected way.

Think About It

- Who are today's "misleaders"?
- How trustworthy are today's leaders?
- Do today's rulers do God's work?
- What responsibilities and challenges do you face in this world?

12

ARE HOLY WARS LEGITIMATE?

Moses my servant is dead; now therefore arise, go over this
Jordan, you and all this people into the land which I am giving
to them, to the people of Israel. Every place that the sole of
your foot will tread upon I have given to you, as I promised to
Moses. (Joshua 1:3-4)

ON THESE AND similar sayings in the Old Testament, Joshua and
his followers and those living in the modern state of Israel have
based their claim for possession of the land.

Because these sayings occur in the Bible, many Christians
support this Jewish claim to a homeland. These Christians are
called either millenarians or premillenarians. In essence they
believe that the Jews must occupy Palestine in order to fulfill
biblical prophecies which will usher in God's Kingdom and the
last eon.

The first mention of the giving of the Promised Land is with
Abraham. It was not for him to possess. Rather it was for his
descendants of some 700 to 1000 years later to lay claim to this
promise. Joshua is the first Israelite to exercise this promise from
God that had been passed down from generation to generation.

The final form of the Book of Joshua was penned by the Deuteronomists sometime after the fall of the Northern Kingdom of Israel in 722 BCE and before the discovery of the law scrolls found in the Temple in 622 BCE. Before the Book of Joshua was put into this form, it existed in song or ballad form. Those men representing the Deuteronomists were from the priestly class who emphasized adherence to the Law and reform of worship. The priests claimed to be the link or intermediary between God and the people. Thus, they were an extremely powerful group.

The book of Joshua is not a history book. It is a theological book. It witnesses to Israel's faith and understanding in a God who intends to establish God's kingly rule upon earth. The Deuteronomists revised Israel's history to express this point of view. They reinterpreted historical events in terms of obedience, divine judgment, retribution, and sometimes mercy. At this point in the Israelite's theological development, God is viewed as a God of election or covenant, a God who enters human history, and a God of Holy War.

God as represented in the Book of Joshua is almost unrecognizable today. Christians and Jews do not believe in a God of War as did the early Israelites. It is books like the Book of Joshua that cause people to turn away from Judaism and Christianity. People cannot believe that God would sanction any war and the total annihilation of men, women, and children no matter whom they might be. We are all God's children. Yet today's Islamic terrorists believe God sanctions their war against those people whom they consider infidels. We need to remember that often history is written, rewritten, reconceived, and edited by the victors and influenced by whatever philosophical or theological position of rightness or justification in which they believe.

Biblical scholars dispute the military success with which Joshua met. Many of the accounts reported in the Book of Joshua are considered legend. Legends are an important part of the oral traditions of a people. They are told partly to inspire the next generation and partly to explain the origins of traditions and the viewpoint of the people.

The Interpreter's Bible suggests that the number of villages and cities taken by outright battle was probably small. The Hebrews lacked the military might to take the populous and relatively well-defended cities of Canaan.

It is estimated that the conquest of Canaan may have taken at least two centuries. In actuality, not all inhabitants were destroyed as depicted in the Book of Joshua. The Israelites lived side by side with them. There was some intermarriage and pagan worship as a result of this living with the Canaanites. The most desirable land was not conquered by the Israelites. In fact, most of the Israelites lived in the less desirable hill country.

It was David who finally conquered all enemies and unified the people under a monarchy. At the time of Joshua, there was already living in the land a dispossessed group of Hebrews known as Habiru and commonly considered from the same ancestry as the Hebrews that came out of Egypt. These people lived in and around the Canaanites city states.

The Israelites accepted these dispossessed people as one of their own as soon as they had purified themselves ritually and covenanted to accept God and God's law. Yahwism, or belief in the God of Israel, offered everyone acceptance, community, identity, and deliverance. This subjective feeling of belonging and loyalty by this dispossessed group helped form them into a close-knit group against all other groups. It is believed that many of the cities that fell during these 200 years of attempted occupation by the Israelites fell because of these dispossessed people's identification with Yahwism and their internal assistance in defeating their overlords.

The Israelites are an exclusive group who believed God fights and wins their battles if they are obedient to God. No such self-understanding existed in the Canaanite population. The psychological impact of this belief is awesome. Rahab, the harlot who hides Joshua's spies, conveys the fear that the Israelites' theology instills in her people. She says:

> I know that the Lord has given you the land, and that the fear of you has fallen upon us, and that all the inhabitants of the land melt away before you. For we have heard how the Lord dried up the water of the Red Sea before you when you came out of Egypt, and what you did to the two kings of the Amorites that were beyond the Jordan...whom you utterly destroyed. And as soon as we heard it, our hearts melted, and there was no courage left in any man, because of you; for the Lord your God is he who is God in heaven above and on earth beneath. (Joshua 2:10-11)

Soon after the spies return to Joshua, the Israelites sanctify themselves in preparation for crossing the Jordan River. This process of sanctification tells us that Joshua and his followers believed this war to be a Holy War. The Levitical priests carry the Ark of the Covenant into the Jordan River. The Ark is the token of God's presence among them and believed to have contained the stone tablets on which the Ten Commandments were written. The waters stop flowing, and the people pass over the dry riverbed. Archaeologists believe that the waters stopped 18 miles north of Jericho at Adam due to a landslide. Similar landslides have occurred over the centuries which stopped this flow of water for a period of time. When the priests and the Ark leave the Jordan River, the river fills up again. Just imagine the impact of this dry-bed crossing had on the already frightened people in Jericho.

Theologically, the Israelites interpreted their crossing of the Jordan River as God's divine act in their history. Not only is their God a God of war but also a God who controls nature.

In holy wars all inhabitants are killed so as to prohibit any contact between diverse peoples. With no contact between the different inhabitants, there would be no exchange of faiths and cultures. Most of the time all gold, silver, bronze, and iron were given to God. All other wealth of the city and its inhabitants are destroyed and burned. Burning of bodies would prevent pestilence from occurring.

Joshua's holy war begins with the priests and all the Israelites marching around the city for six days with seven priests blowing seven ram's horns. The number seven indicates perfection, completeness, and consummation. Also note the use of the number seven with seven priests, seven trumpets, seven days, seven circuits of the walls on the seventh day. The ram's horns blown by the priests had a ceremonial rather than a martial purpose. For them, this was a religious war, not a military war. The constant blowing of the ceremonial horns served not only to remind the Israelites of the spiritual nature of their conquest, but also to strike terror into the hearts of their adversaries. This awesome sound, persisting day after day, must have suggested supernatural power to the Jericho inhabitants.

On the seventh day, when the priests and people have completed their seventh trip around the city and the priests blow their horns, Joshua orders them to shout. Then the walls of Jericho crumble. Archaeologists say that the earth quaked at that time. Joshua and his men storm the city and destroy it and its inhabitants except for Rahab and her family.

Often as we read the Bible, we wonder why God is supposedly saying certain things. Did you know that God is not speaking directly to an individual? Instead that individual goes to a priest to get a word from God. A priest gets his answers to questions by using the Urim and Thummim. These are lots, or flat stones, white on one side and black on the other. If both fell white side upwards the answer to any questions was in the affirmative, if black side upwards then the answer is in the negative. If they differed, no reply was given to the question.

In other words, the priest or whoever possessed these lots

would ask a question, throw the stones, and obtain an answer to their question based on the throw of the stones and the way in which they fell. I do not believe that God ordered the wholesale destruction of Jericho. Joshua and his followers "thought" God ordered it where in fact that decision was probably based on the way the Urim and Thummim fell.

Before we take the Book of Joshua literally and believe all that it says, we need to remind ourselves of its author's purpose in writing it. That purpose was to legitimatize holy wars in the name of Yahweh whom the people believed gave them the Promised Land. The authors also wished to put more power into the hands of the priestly class.

In the New Testament, we learn from Jesus that no wars are legitimate and authorized by God. Nor should the Book of Revelation with its emphasis on Armageddon and the second coming overshadow the truths found in the gospels. War and genocide are not the solution to problems arising from the intermingling and coexistence of various cultures and diverse beliefs. Everybody is entitled to a place under the sun. We are all God's children. The need for militarism comes not from God but from people like the Ayatollahs and Islamic terrorists' leaders who misrepresent God's will and use it to legitimate their rule over others to do their warped bidding.

It is important that we have an understanding of the entire Bible in light of the various parts, author's purposes, and theological understandings. Only then will we be able to understand and interpret the smaller units and possible embellishments. We will then be able to compare the Book of Joshua to what Jesus says in the Sermon on the Mount and realize the overriding importance of what Jesus says.

Blessed are the peacemakers, for they shall be called sons of God. (Matthew 5:7)

Think About It:

- What are your thoughts about holy wars?
- Are they justified? What makes you think so?
- How can people stop holy wars and/or should they?
- Do you believe God ordered Joshua and the Israelites to take, destroy, and kill all the inhabitants of Jericho? Why?
- Why did story tellers create the religious validation for holy wars?

13

JUST WAR THEORY

In 2003, Saddam Hussein spoke to his people on Baghdad Radio. He opened with a quotation from the Koran calling the faithful to keep God's covenant. Hussein joins the Iraqi fight to the Arab struggle against the infidel. Hussein declared a holy war. He said:

> We in Iraq will be the faithful and obedient servants of God, struggling for his sake to raise the banner of truth and justice....The valiant Iraqi men and women will not allow the army of atheism, treachery, and hypocrisy realize their stupid hope that the war would only last a few days or weeks....The fact remains that the great divine reinforcement is our source of power and effectiveness....Then the skies in the Arab homeland will appear in a new color and a sun of new hope will shine over them and over our nation and on all the good men whose bright lights will not be overcome by the darkness in the hearts of the infidels, the Zionists, and the treacherous, shameful rulers, such as the traitor Fahd.

From Hussein's speech we gather that he believes God is on his side. It is natural in any war to call upon God. But the US Civil War taught us that God does not fight for either side, because no side is all good and the other side all evil. The same holds true today.

Saddam Hussein was calling his people to carry out a holy war. Let me quickly review the roots of holy war and then the Islamic version that grew out of our Judeo/Christian heritage.

Old Testament covenant theology dominates the Judeo/Christian version of holy war that declares loyalty to God will bring blessings and the land, a place where people can live, enjoy life, and prosper as God's people. Disloyalty to God will bring curses and dispossession.

The presupposition to holy war is stated in Exodus 15:3 when Moses and Miriam sing a song of praise to God. They and the newly freed Hebrew slaves crossed the Sea of Reeds safely and are safe from Pharaoh's soldiers. They believe that God is a warrior. Coupled with this conviction is the confidence that God has power to win victories for them.

A necessary prerequisite to a belief in a holy war is an uncompromising trust in the power of God to give the victory. The Exodus from Egypt is the premier example of God's deliverance of the people. The battle of Jericho is another example.

Later, in prophetic times, this quality of trust is missing. Instead, people trust in their wealth, their armies, and in foreign alliances. Isaiah condemns these beliefs. He says:

> Woe to those who go down to Egypt for help and rely on horses, who trust in chariots because they are many and in horsemen because they are very strong, but do not look to the Holy One of Israel or consult the Lord! (Isa. 31:1f)

Consultation with God is a necessary prelude to Holy War. No step could be taken without divine approval. God's will became known to people through dreams and the casting of the Urim and Thummim.

Defense of Israelite territory against foreign invasion was considered grounds for a holy war. Armed invasion was a violation of God's covenant with Israel. The land belonged to God. The people believed they were defending God when they defended the land. It was God that unified the people in a cause greater than themselves. The only exception to foreigners invading their land is when the people believed God sent the invaders to punish the people for their evil ways. For instance, the prophet Amos says:

> Thus says the Lord: For three transgressions of Israel, and for four, I will not revoke the punishment; because they sell the righteous for silver, and the needy for a pair of shoes—they that trample the head of the poor into the dust of the earth, and turn aside the way of the afflicted. (Amos 8)

The most offensive part of holy war is the *herem*. That is when the people believe that God is instructing them to kill all inhabitants so as to prohibit any contact between them and the Israelites. With no contact between the people of different cultures, there is no exchange of faiths and cultures, thereby keeping their faith pure and unadulterated. Everyone and everything is to be destroyed except for gold and silver which are to be given to the Lord.

Holy war ideology became an integral part of Old Testament theology. It emphasized the sovereignty of God, God's initiative, God's concern for God's people and God's activity as deliverer and preserver.

The early Christian church spiritualized the holy war and saw in it a struggle against sin, Satan, and the demonic forces of the cosmos. Early Christians believed the decisive battle against evil forces was won in the death and resurrection of Jesus. Our hymns reflect this spiritualized holy war mentality. We sing:

Onward Christian soldiers,
Marching as to war,
With the cross of Jesus
Going on before,
Christs the royal Master
Leads against the foe,
Forward into battle,
See his banners go.

Now let us look at Islam. Islam has its roots in Judaism, Christianity, Zoroastrianism, and Hinduism. Islam began in the seventh century in Arabia as a result of the preaching and teaching of the Prophet Muhammad who insisted upon strict monotheism. Islam recognizes a whole series of prophets including Noah, Moses, and Jesus. But Muhammad is considered God's last supreme prophet.

Islam's equivalent to our covenant theology is the Five Pillars of Faith, the Koran, and the jihad or holy war. These impose a religious duty on the people to spread Islam. There are four ways to fulfill this duty of spreading Islam. They are by the heart through purification of one's spirit, by the tongue and hand by supporting what is right and correcting what is wrong, and by waging war physically against unbelievers and enemies of the Islamic faith. Therefore, we should not under estimate Islamic evangelical zeal.

Exceptions to their universal adherence to this Five Pillars of faith are granted Islam's ancestors which includes Christians and Jews provided they either embrace Islam or submit themselves to

Islamic rule and pay a tax on savings and land. If both options are rejected, jihad or holy war is declared.

Modern and more liberal Islam similar to moderate and liberal Christianity places special emphasis on waging war with one's inner self. Modern Islam does not sanction war with other nations except as a defensive measure when Islam is placed in danger. The object of the jihad is not the conversion of individuals to Islam but rather the gaining of political control over the collective affairs of societies to run them in accordance with the principles of Islam. In Iran with the overthrow of the Shah, Islamic rule was reestablished. The jihad was a success. Muslims forbid conversions by force. Conversions are to occur as a by-product of the political process when the power structure passes into the hands of the Muslim communities.

As we know, Islam and Christianity are divided into numerous sects. Many sects think they have the only private line to God. These super Christian and super Islamic sects wage war against their own who hold a different understanding of their faith. Examples are easy to find. We have the Catholics versus the Protestants in Northern Ireland. We have the Shiite Muslims versus the rest of the Islamic sects. In the US, we do not wage a physical war but we do have our war of words and nerves between the fundamentalists and those of a more moderate or liberal orientation.

Holy wars still exist today especially in the Middle East where no just war exists. Yemen civilian casualties in 2019 were estimated to be more than 17,500, a quarter of which were women and children. Over 3500 males have disappeared. Hospitals, schools, market places, factories, and homes have been bombed by Saudi-led coalition planes. The US, the UK, and France are complicit in war crimes through their arms and air plane sales to Saudi Arabia.

Nations have the right to self-defense against foreign aggression. In 1993, the US Catholic Conference said: "Force may be used only to correct a grave, public evil, i.e., aggression or massive violation of the basic human rights of whole populations."

How should we go forward today? Let me list a few of my thoughts.

1. We need to call dictators' and authoritarians' bluff. They are not eligible to call a holy war. Recognize that their personal motives are political, economic, and territorial.

2. We need to address the Palestinian problem. Until this problem is addressed and resolved satisfactorily, there will be no peace in the Middle East. The world community should insist the Israeli government negotiate with the Palestinians in resolving the issues regarding the West Bank and Gaza. If this problem is not resolved, every Arab head of state or terrorist leader can use this problem as a rallying call to arms.

3. We should not demonize Arabs. They are people just like ourselves. They have feelings, loved ones, families, and survival needs, too. Do not let the press or the mass media demonize them. Also, many Arabs are Christians. When I was in Israel in 1980, I was a guest in a Christian Palestinian home. Another guest in that home was the Anglican Bishop of Jerusalem. These Palestinians were pleading their case. They told us how their homes have been taken from them without any compensation, how they cannot own property, have no citizenship status, limited employment opportunities, and no future. They were pleading with US Christians to help resolve the Palestinian issue which divides peace-loving people.

Forty-one years later nothing has changed in their favor.

4. We need to help the Arabs understand us and help them to become modern states minus the hedonism that goes along with modern secular states. The Christian community lives in the secular world but does not participate in what is immoral and ungodly. Muslim and Christian Arabs should be allowed to do likewise.

5. We need to recommit ourselves to the Lord, examine the wrong we have done, ask for forgiveness, and be spiritually renewed.

In conclusion, the Saddam Husseins of the world can call upon God or say they speak for God all they want. They are frauds and not men of God. They are murderers of thousands and jailers of thousands more. They destroy our environment with ecological warfare and try to intimidate the free world.

Our government and armed forces are doing what they can to protect us and other vulnerable nations. We may not agree with all their methods, but they are in possession of more facts than we. We have to trust their honest efforts to make the best possible decisions. No decision will ever be perfect. All decisions will be open to criticism and second guessing. In times of crisis, it is important to stand behind our government, our NATO alliance members, and our men and women in uniform. It is a time to pray for God's mercy, wisdom, and enlightenment on how to stop wars and live in peace.

Think About It

- What are your thoughts about holy wars?

- Why do you or don't you believe in a just war theory?
- How should our country react to weapons of mass destruction?
- Why should we withdraw our troops from Iraq, Afghanistan, and other places?

14

WHERE IS GOD?

WE READ in I Samuel 4:11f and 5:6-12 of the battle between the well-armed and invading Philistine army and of its defeat of the ill-equipped and untrained army made up of Israelite farmers and peasants. The Israelite tribal leaders believed their defeat was due to their lack of religious fervor. Therefore, they fetched the Ark of the Covenant from Shiloh to carry into battle with them.

This plan did not work. The Israelites were defeated, and the Ark of the Covenant was captured by the Philistines. It was offered and placed before their god Dagon who fell down and broke into pieces before the Ark. Also, at that time the Philistines were experiencing the bubonic plague which they believed was caused by the presence of the Ark. Therefore, they returned the Ark to the Israelites. Historians believe the Philistine cities were overrun by mice that carried the bubonic plague germ.

Whenever I read these scripture readings from I Samuel, I think of the movie *Raiders of the Lost Ark* with Harrison Ford. It is a story of intrigue and greed. Harrison Ford plays the role of Indiana Jones, an archeology professor, who is hired by the U.S. government to find the lost Ark of the Covenant before Hitler's Nazis can find it and obtain its awesome powers. There are parallels to I Samuel's description of the Israelite battles and outcomes with the Philistines. Have the boundaries between religion and magic been crossed?

Are we dealing with some Old Testament science fiction story or did the events described in this story actually happen? If the Ark had the magical powers the Israelites believed it had, why did they lose their battles with the Philistines and their Holy Ark?

We are uncertain as to exactly what the Ark represented. It was an oblong box dating from the Israelites' days in the wilderness. In the Exodus accounts, the Ark was believed to be an empty throne on which God sat. The Israelites believed that wherever the Ark was God would always be fully present. God's presence in the Ark was always regarded as bestowing blessings.

The account in I Samuel is believed to have been first recorded in writing by some unknown historian in Solomon's court. The final editing of this story occurred during the Israelites' exile in Babylonia some 360-400 years later.

These editors were from the Deuteronomic School who also shaped the books of Judges, Samuel, and Kings. The Deuteronomist had a different idea about the Ark than did the writers of the Exodus accounts. They did not believe that the Ark contained God's throne or God. They believed the Ark contained the stone tablets on which the Ten Commandments were written and nothing more. It seems that the Israelites as well as the Philistines are confusing reality with the symbol which the Ark represents. It was not an idol to be worshipped nor the equivalent of a magic wand.

The Ark may be the symbol for God, but the Ark is not in reality God. Also, the Ark is not a magic box. It is not a security blanket. The Philistines and Israelites invested in and projected on the Ark their perceptions of God and the terror these perceptions generate within people.

We cannot explain the death of 70 men who peered into the

Ark. Perhaps they had to pay with their lives as did the men in the *Raiders of the Lost Ark* who peered into something which had been set aside as holy. Their act was one of desecration and presumption. If the Exodus theology dominated the writer of these stories, then it was understood that anyone who attempted to look on the face of God would die.

The theological implications of this story are twofold.

1. The Ark was not a magic box. It could not save the people from their troubles. God dramatically says "no" to any form of manipulation or idolatry.
2. God does not dwell in or is enthroned on the Ark. God dwells everywhere and cannot be located in one place.

Most Christians agree with the Deuteronomists' position. God's presence is everywhere and all encompassing. People may try to capture God in a certain place or thing, but God in Jesus has shown us in no uncertain terms that God will not be contained anywhere or any place as demonstrated by Jesus' empty tomb and resurrection. God is not anchored to a time nor place but lives and moves throughout all time and places.

Rabbi Aaron Goldscheider believes the Ark contained the shattered pieces of the two tablets that Moses threw on the ground when he reacted to the Israelites' worship of the golden calf. These pieces were put in the Ark along with the new tablets given by God. He writes:

> The two sets of tablets in the Ark offer a striking metaphor. Namely that brokenness and wholeness coexist side by side, even in Judaism's holiest spot—in the heart of the Holy Ark... Brokenness and wholeness coexist side by side in the chambers of the heart.

We need to face our special time with faith, optimism,

brokenness, and wholeness. God provides us with minimum protection. God does not give us an Ark to cling to. But God will give us maximum support. If we have faith in God and ourselves, then we can face all adversities as well as joys as God's people. God wants us to grow in faith, trust, and in the fruits of the Spirit. God wants us to stretch our minds and hearts until they are as wide as God's universe.

Think About It

- Have you found God? If so, how did you do it?
- If you have not found God, why haven't you?
- Do you believe God is at your beckon call? Why or why not?
- What expectations may God have for you?
- Have the stories about the Ark crossed boundaries between religion and magic?
- Do you believe you can find the presence of God through your struggles and tests?

15

LONGINGS

GOD REVEALED little of Godself to Moses at the burning bush. Over the years Moses came to know, trust, and love God. This process was a gradual, unfolding one that occurred over many, many years.

Today, some people would like to learn more about God, but they want God to be sold to them like a 30-second commercial wherein they can make a quick decision whether to buy or not to buy into the notion of God. People are in a frantic rush seeking the good life, the perfect mate, success for their children and themselves, and fame and fortune. They make quick decisions on little shreds of information that will have a lasting impact on their lives.

Our culture concentrates on meaningful self-expression. It insists we be something special. This drive for self-expression leads some people to unhealthy competition, bitterness, anger, hopelessness, and no happiness.

Our problem is that we tend to over-expect today. We believe that every hunger within us needs to be met. We stand before life and love in a greedy posture and with unrealistic expectations.

We forget that life for us will always be an unfinished symphony because we are not the Creator.

We buy into idealized and non-Christian visions that falsely assure us of heaven on earth. We let these visions drive our behavior, manner of relating to others, and our spiritual lives. We replace God with minor deities of our own making to whom we dutifully pay homage.

We seek the world's vision of success rather than a deep, abiding relationship with God. We seek novelty and spiritual gurus who claim to possess the key to happiness, success, and great fortune rather than study Holy Scripture to unlock the riches, truths, and revelations of God found therein. We avoid worshipping God together as a faith community because we do not have time for it. And we do not want to be bound by God's commandments and think we can get by claiming ignorance of them.

There is a story about two young boys who went fishing. They caught four nice trout, but it took most of the day to do it. As the sun went down, they chose to use the railroad tracks as a short-cut home. Neither boy had ever taken this route. But one boy heard that it was easy if you did not mind crossing a series of narrow trestles that spanned some deep gorges. The boys came to the first bridge, just wide enough for a train or two foolish boys to cross. They crossed the second bridge without incident.

By the time they came to the last trestle, it was too dark to see even their feet on a starless night. As they were crossing it, a bright light blinded them. A locomotive was rounding the curve and coming towards them. The frightened boys turned and started back, but they could not hop from tie to tie quickly enough in the darkness. There was only one thing to do. They laid their fishing poles and fish across the timbers between the rails. They slipped between the ties and hung by their arms beneath the tracts. The train roared overhead, knocking cinders in their eyes and nearly shaking them loose. The cars kept coming.

When the last car finally passed, they tried to pull themselves up, but their arms were too tired to do so. So, in the darkness, they hung there and took turns yelling for help. They could not last much longer. The boys whimpered, and one boy wished he had been a better boy and promised God to be a better boy if … Suddenly, a small beam of light from under the bridge approached. "What's happening here?" a voice called out. And two eyes looked straight into the boys' eyes. The boy thought: "Oh my God, it is God!"

The voiced continued: "What are you dumb boys doing hanging from these tracks?" And the man shined his lantern at the boys' feet which was ten inches above the ground.

Similar to these boys, we often misjudge our circumstances. Jesus tells us that there is a creed by which we should live. This creed is known as the Great Love Commandment where there are no short cuts or blind alleyways that will lead us to wholeness in life. Wholeness in life only comes through our knowledge and love of God and obedience to God. Jesus establishes love as the foundation of Christian faith and life.

Modern-day people consider themselves to be pretty sophisticated. Many choose not to be taken in by the claims and demands of Christianity. Paul, Christ's missionary to the Gentiles, encountered the counterpart to modern sophisticates when he entered Athens, a university town. Paul confronted the Greeks and indirectly you and me. Paul is unimpressed by the best of pagan culture. He views Athens as a wasteland full of idols. He is misunderstood by the religious and philosophical leaders of the day, namely the Jews, Epicureans, and Stoics. They thought he was a preacher of foreign deities. Their curiosity spurred them to take Paul into the middle of the Athenian marketplace known as the Areopagus. All the intellectuals gathered around him. They thought Paul may have something new to add to their pagan world views.

Paul flattered his audience by calling them spiritual seekers.

He observed from their numerous temples and statues that they worshiped many gods. Paul believed they possessed a yearning for the God whom only Holy Scripture, the prophets, and Jesus can disclose. Then Paul moved to assert:

> The God who made the world and everything in it is Lord of heaven and earth. God does not live in shrines made by human hands, nor is God served by human hands. God gives to all mortals, life and breath and all things. (Acts 17:24-25)

Paul continued to say that we are God's children. We belong to the created order made by God our creator. God is not an idol of gold or silver made by human hands. God is not an old man in the sky. God cannot be fully defined or known by finite creatures.

Old Testament professor Walter Brueggemann once said that one thing we do learn from scripture and experience is that **God is a holy power with a moral purpose that is non-negotiable.**

Paul told his listeners and us today that God has overlooked our time of ignorance and now calls us to repent and believe in the gospel. The natural world informs us up to a point something about whom God is. But in nature things grow, decline, die, and decay. Death ends their life cycle. But God is eternal. God is in charge of the universe. God reverses the natural order of life and death through the resurrection of Jesus. When the people heard Paul talk about Jesus' resurrected life, some mocked him while others believed.

Theologian William Willimon says:

> The God whom Paul proclaims is not just another option for human devotion, not an accommodating God content to be one among many. The God who sent the Christ is still the Holy One of Israel, a jealous God without rivals, an exclusive lover who tolerates no competition—money, sex, philosophical ideals and

institutions. God fiercely judges all idols made by hands or minds of men.

We meet God in Christ who in turn gives us our identity, our roots, our past, our present, and our future. And God in Christ gives us the Great Love Commandment which should govern our lives. Jesus says:

'Hear, O Israel: the Lord our God, the Lord is one; you shall love the Lord you God with all your heart, and with all your soul, and with all your mind, and with all your strength.' The second is this, 'You shall love your neighbor as yourself.' There is no other commandment greater than these. (Mark 12:29-31)

Think About It

- Do you believe we live in a pagan culture? If so, what makes you think so?
- Why is success important to you?
- Why do you agree or disagree with what William Willimon has to say about God?
- What do you think of Walter Brueggemann's statement about God?
- What are your thoughts on the Great Love Commandment?

16

VALIDATION

Jesus also told this parable to some who trusted in themselves that they were righteous and regarded others with contempt. "Two men went up to the temple to pray, one a Pharisee and the other a tax collector. The Pharisee, standing by himself, was praying thus, 'God, I thank you that I am not like other people: thieves, rogues, adulterers, or even like this tax collector. I fast twice a week: I give a tenth of all my income.' But the tax collector, standing far off, would not even look up to heaven, but was beating his breast saying, 'God, be merciful to me, a sinner!' I tell you, this man went down to his home justified rather than the other; for all who exalt themselves will be humbled, but all who humble themselves will be exalted." (Luke 18:9-14)

THESE DAYS many people want to be in the headlines. They seek validation of their worthiness for whatever they do, say, give, and/or wear. It may begin in childhood when they want the attention and praise from their parents over a rival sibling. As a child grows, he wants the gold star from a teacher. If he participates in team activities, he must perform well so as to benefit and be accepted by the team. And on and on it goes.

Often loneliness drives people's behavior. They need to be part of something bigger than themselves to validate their lives. They may give generously to fund raisers that publicly recognize their generosity. But some may still be lonely.

So, what happens to the loner and non-achiever? How can his life be validated? Can he make his mark in this world? And what extremes will he go to? Shall he be a mass shooter or join a terrorist group to feel important? Or should he put self aside and volunteer to help the hungry, the poor, the homeless, the refugee, the asylum seeker, persecuted minorities, and other vulnerable people?

Jesus' parable of the Pharisee and tax collector suggests that you should not tell God how great you are and expect God to endorse your self-esteem. Nor should you expect the same from the world. Instead, we should approach God and life like the tax collector with humility and contrition with no claims to superior rights.

Think About It

- What do you think God wants you to do with your life and will you do it?
- Do you let other people define who you are? If so, why?
- How important is it to you to be validated by others?
- Do you know anyone like the Pharisee and the tax collector?
- How do you interact with them?
- What can you do to help the lonely, the excluded, and the bullied?

17

A BRIEF HISTORY FROM MOSES TO JESUS

AROUND THE YEAR 1250 BCE, Moses led the descendants of Jacob out of Egyptian slavery and into the wilderness. They wandered in the wilderness for 40 years. During this time, they formed themselves into a nation, and received the Mosaic Law, which they promised to keep.

About 1210 BCE, Joshua led the Israelites into Canaan. During the first two centuries of Israelite life in Canaan, Judges ruled the twelve tribes. The major theme in the book of Judges is **To Be Strong, a Nation Must be Loyal to God**. During this time, the Israelites went through a recurring cycle of sin, national punishment for their sins by God, repentance, forgiveness and deliverance by God.

At about 1020 BCE, Saul was crowned the Israelites first king. His reign lasted 30 years. Saul spent most of his time fighting the enemies of Israel, especially the Philistines.

Upon the death of Saul, David became king of the two southern Israelite tribes. After seven years, the 10 northern tribes made him king over them, too. David's reign then lasted 40 years. As king, David limited the autonomy of the individual tribes and centralized his government in Jerusalem. His court collected taxes and dispensed justice over all of Canaan. The nation shifted from an agrarian/tribal society to a class-stratified and non-equalitarian society. David enforced his law by maintaining a standing army. During his reign, Jerusalem became the Israelites' "Holy City."

Under Solomon, David's son by Bathseba, the nation reached its greatest glory. However, the seeds of its destruction were sown as well. Solomon overspent and overtaxed his people and enslaved many of his subjects to build palaces and pagan temples for his numerous wives. Solomon ruled for 39 years.

After Solomon's death, the nation was divided in two. Judah, the Southern Kingdom, was ruled by Solomon's son Rehoboam. Israel, the Northern Kingdom, was ruled by Jeroboam, Solomon's former project supervisor. The two kingdoms were never reunited.

Prophets now became the conscience of the two nations. The prophets no longer considered the Israelite kings to be anointed by God and did not regard them as the nation's spiritual leaders. Elijah was a pre-classical prophet. He challenged Ahab, Jezebel, and the ruling families in the northern Kingdom. Amos, a classical or writing prophet, was also a prophet to Israel. The Assyrian army defeated Israel in 722 BCE and annexed it to the Assyrian Empire.

Judah, the Southern Kingdom, survived for another 135 years. The principal prophets during this time were Isaiah and Jeremiah. Judah fell in 587 BCE to the Babylonians.

The prophets warned that the Jewish people's covenant with God was being threatened, surpassed, and superseded because of their lack of faith and trust in God. They also criticized the Israelites for their wrong relationships with their neighbors. The prophets warned the people that God would abandon them to their enemies if they did not repent. After other nations did indeed defeat and punish the Jewish people, the classical prophets held out the hope that a remnant of the Jewish nation would survive and rise again.

While the Jews were in exile in Babylonia, Isaiah II became their principal prophet. He preached that the role of the Jewish people was to bring God's light to the world. When Cyrus of Persia conquered Babylonia, he allowed the Jews to return home to rebuild their homeland. Nehemiah and Ezra were the principal prophets during this Restoration.

In 332 BCE, Alexander the Great conquered the Jews. He began the Hellenization of the area, that is, the subjection of Jewish to Greek culture. When Alexander died nine years later, his conquered territory was divided. The Ptolemaic dynasty and the Seleucid dynasty—both remnants of Alexander's Greek empire—fought for control. Each dynasty ruled at various times. In 198 BCE, Seleucid Antiochus III defeated Ptolemy V. In 175 BCE, Antiochus IV Epiphanes became the ruler. In 167 BCE he banned all Jewish religious practices, desecrated the Jerusalem Temple, and forced the Jews to adopt the Greek language, culture, and worship.

The Jewish people revolted against Antiochus IV's oppression. Judas Maccabeus led the revolt and successfully rid the country of the Seleucids. His family ruled until 63 BCE. Internal family strife caused the family to seek Roman support for their rule. Pompey took advantage of this division, captured Jerusalem, and placed all Israelites under Roman rule. The Romans set up their puppet governor, Antipater, Herod the Great, over them. Upon his death, his son, Herod Antipater, assumed power and was made king of the Jews. When Herod died in 4 CE, his realm was divided among his three sons. Herod Antipas ruled Galilee.

Into this world of military might and oppression Jesus was born.

Think About It

- List the themes that dominate the historical period from Moses to Jesus.
- What similarities exist during this historical time period?
- What similarities exist today?

18

HIGH HOPES

SIX MONTHS after the angel Gabriel's visit to Zachariah announcing that his aged wife Elizabeth will conceive a son, Gabriel visits a Jewish peasant maiden named Mary. He tells her that she is favored and blessed among women and has been chosen by God to conceive and bear a son whom she will call Jesus. Gabriel's visit to Mary is known as the *Annunciation.*

Of course, Mary wonders how this can occur as she is a virgin. Gabriel tells her "The Holy Spirit will come upon you, and the power of the Most High will overshadow you; therefore, the child to be born will be holy; he will be called Son of God." Mary then says, "Here am I, the servant of the Lord; let it be with me according to your word." (Luke 1:35-38)

The term *overshadow* does not refer to divine sexual activity as found in Greek myths of gods impregnating women. By using the Greek term for *overshadow,* Luke emphasizes the miraculous circumstances of Jesus' conception and removes any thoughts of sexual intercourse. The emphasis here is that Jesus has human and divine origins.

In other words, the entire birth story is not a matter of biology. It is a matter of religious truths and beliefs. Mary represents the faithful of Israel who respond to God's call for humble loving service. Whatever your belief or acceptance or rejection of these birth narratives, all gospels emphasize that these nativity stories are legendary, not historical. No eyewitnesses were present at the moment of conception. But the doctrine of the virgin birth is of great theological importance. Mary's role and the Holy Spirit initiative as given to us in the birth narratives assures believers that Jesus is of both human and divine origin. This whole virgin birth matter is not a matter of biology. It is a matter of theology. These nativity stories want to make it clear that Jesus is God who comes to us in the flesh. His incarnation is a new creative act and revelation by God.

Marian piety developed during the Middle Ages. Mary became the role model for obedience, chastity, and poverty. Pious devotees venerated Mary and prepared the way for church dogma to follow. Church leaders reasoned that Mary had to be without sin and was born free of original sin in order to claim that Jesus was born sinless and of a sinless woman. Therefore, in 1854, Pope Pius IX proposed the dogma of the *Immaculate Conception* (freedom from the stain of original sin)

- Without a consensus from church leaders,
- Without proof from scripture and tradition, and
- Without any proof from antiquity.

Almost 100 years after the dogma of the Immaculate Conception in 1950, the Roman Catholic Church declared the *Assumption of the Virgin Mary.* That means that Mary, upon her death, her body and soul were assumed or ascended into heaven. During early New Testament times, Mary, the mother of Jesus Christ, had no preferred status. Yet in the modern age, Mary occupies a very important place among Roman Catholics. In fact, Roman Catholic doctrine insists on four important doctrines that believers must accept for their salvation. These are:

- That Mary is the Mother of God
- That she remained a virgin all her life
- That Mary was immaculately conceived
- That she was bodily assumed into heaven.

Into this world of military might and oppression, Jesus was born. His times were dark times. Mary and Joseph were subjected to the fickleness of unrestrained power and rulers trying to maintain their control at the expense of the masses. Religious Jews looked to their religious leaders for help and guidance in how to live under foreign domination. Many religious leaders were coopted by the Romans and used their positions to maintain the status quo for the Romans and themselves. These religious leaders tried to reduce God to a patron saint rather than recognize God as the sovereign ruler of their lives.

Mary and Joseph are representative of the common people. They and the rest of the nation are required by Emperor Augustus to register in their hometowns. So, Joseph and Mary had to travel the dirt roads to Bethlehem because Joseph was descended from the house and family of David. Mary, Joseph, and thousands of other people were traveling the roads to their places of birth.

They and other poor people had to rest and sleep alongside the road unprotected by any form of shelter. The only food they had to eat was what they carried with them or were able to buy.

A common part of the scenery along these roads were crucified Jewish nationalists known as Zealots. No one could come to their aid. No one could remove them from their crosses. All legal rights were suspended for non-Romans.

Yet Mary and Joseph faced these realities and the extremities of life unafraid. They had hope in a hopeless world. They had a secret that no one else knew. Into this bleak world and in an unsanitary stable with no human comforts, Mary gives birth to Jesus. Through her, hope enters the world. Hope is wonder and mystery yet unknown. Hope shapes the future.

In our lives, most of us have serious problems that persist and do not seem to go away. Some of us try to deal with our problems with a sort of magical hope. Magical hope is based on illusion and arises out of a desire for wish fulfillment not based in reality. For instance, I may wish to be ten years younger, taller, and the mother of 10 children. These hopes are magical hopes not based in reality.

In contrast to magical hope is Christian hope. Christian hope is not divorced from present reality but centers more on it. Christian hope embodies an "in-spite-of" quality. Christian hope implies confidence that something good is going to take place, although it has not yet happened. Those of us who accept the harshness of reality can have the same hope that Mary and Joseph had. We can have a sure and certain hope in God and in God's promises. That hope can free us from our prison of gloom and despair and cause us to work towards overcoming the trials and tribulations of life.

Everybody has a story about how Christian hope can change lives. Charles Allen in his book *God's Psychiatry* tells how the Allied armies in WWII gathered up homeless children and cared for them. But at night, the children were restless and afraid. A psychologist hit upon a solution. He gave each child a slice of bread to hold, and the child would go to sleep immediately knowing that he or she would have something to eat the next day. The line in the Lord's Prayer "Give us this day our daily bread" has profound significance even for little children.

Hope is an SOS signal. A person does not hope if there is nothing wrong or lacking, just as a ship does not dash off an SOS signal except as a call for help. Hope says two things about our human condition. First, we are aware of being in distress even to the point of fearing total shipwreck. And second, we anticipate the possibility of rescue, searching the horizon from where help might come.

The heart of the problem for too many of us is the loss of confidence and the absence of hope. Such a loss always leads to despair. And the main problem with despair is that it is self-fulfilling. When we fear the worst, we tend to invite the worst to come. When our heads are down, we cannot see the horizon. New visions and new possibilities only come when we lift our eyes, look ahead and look for God's presence, and God's signature in our lives and in the world.

Christmas tells us to hope in tomorrow. The gospel of Luke tells us that Jesus ushers in a new order which emerges from the old order. Elizabeth, a barren old woman gives birth to John the Baptist. Mary, an innocent but believing young peasant girl, gives birth to Jesus Christ. The shepherds, society's rejects, are the first to be informed of the new order. The old order of enslavement, guilt, judgment, darkness, and hostility gives way to the possibilities of salvation, forgiveness, mercy, light, and peace. God has not and will not be held captive by the old order.

Jesus' birth is only a hope. We will have to wait for Jesus' ministry for the possibilities of hope to be engaged seriously in this world of despair. The old order will not sanction Jesus' ministry. It is too new. It is too threatening. As Luke says: "The chief priest and the scribes and the principal men of the people sought to destroy him." (19:47)

Jesus' actions violate established propriety, reason, and good public order. There is surprise that futures can be given to people who seem to have no future, people who are denied riches, and people who have no reason to laugh. An unmanaged newness and hope enters the world. It cannot be controlled by rulers.

The staggering works of Jesus—feeding, healing, casting out demons, forgiving—happened not to those who held to the old order but to those who yearned for something new because the old order had failed them or squeezed them out. Jesus gave hope and new life to the disinherited.

The Hebrew word for hope has the root meaning of "to twist" or "to twine" and is related to the word spider web. So much of our hoping has this spider web quality to it—this quality of incredible strength out of weakness, of spectacular beauty from the tiny, insignificant, even petty strands of our lives. We live in a network of hopes, each one lending strength to the others, and all of them somehow supporting us, leading us into the future. However, we need to remember that the beautiful spider web has only a few strands supporting the whole. If those strands are cut, the web will fall to the ground. Christian strands are the life-giving strands that connect us to God incarnate in Jesus Christ.

Let us remember that it was out of the silence of despair and the seeming absence of God that hope came into the world.

Jesus' birth tells us never to give up hope. There is nothing to fear but fear itself. If we ask for it, God will give us the courage to face all extremities.

Nor are we to look for the quick fix. God works at God's own timetable not our own. Jesus came to show us a different way to live from the ways of the world. Changes for Jesus and for us will not be sudden. Often, they are slow, gradual, and impercepti-ble. But when we look back over a year, many years, a century or two, we can see the effect of Jesus on the world. The wicked have striven and will continue to strive to have domination over us, but ultimately, they are and will be defeated. It is our job to resist such wickedness. We are God's hands, feet, eyes, and voices. Emmanuel, God with us, is in the world yesterday, today, and tomorrow. No force can rival God.

Let us keep our hopes high. And let us claim our inheritance.

Think About It

- What are your thoughts on Mary, Jesus' mother?
- Why do you suppose the Roman Catholic Church developed the doctrine of the Immaculate Conception and the Assumption of the Virgin Mary?
- What causes you to have hope or no hope in today's world?

19

GOD'S LOVE IS VULNERABLE

THE STRUGGLE between those with power and those who are vulnerable is highlighted in Jesus' life at the time of his birth. (Please read about it in Matthew 2.) It is a struggle between a legitimate and an illegitimate king. Herod is a Roman puppet ruling over an enslaved people. He is not even Jewish. He is of Idumaen stock. Remember his father, Herod Antipater, aided the Romans in their invasion of Israel in 63 BCE.

Matthew tries to emphasize that the baby Jesus is king not only of the Jews but of all people. Before the Israelites switched from a confederacy form of government to a monarchy beginning with Saul, they believed that God was their king and that they needed no earthly king. Jesus becomes God incarnate among them. He is a king that will affect their spiritual lives which no illegitimate king can rule.

The mere fact that Jesus comes as a baby whose life is threatened tells us something about God. Babies are vulnerable. They are totally dependent on their parents for sustenance and protection. God is not forcing God's self on us. God comes as a gift of love. God comes in the flesh as a baby with all its vulnerability. God's love is vulnerable. Israel was not looking for a baby to save them. What could a baby do? They wanted a military leader like David to lead them.

We Christians, too, are only given the security we find in a vulnerable Jesus. We, like Jesus, must confront and fight the evil in this world without armies.

Matthew's gospel says that when Herod heard from the wise men that they wanted to worship the King of the Jews that Herod was troubled and all Jerusalem with him. Perhaps the people in Jerusalem liked the dim light in their lives. Perhaps they shared the same hostility for the light which reveals the darkness of their souls. No one can hide from God's revealing light. At this point in Jesus' life, it is Herod that threatens His life.

God intervenes by warning Joseph in a dream to flee to Egypt with Jesus and Mary. The wise men are also warned not to return to Herod. When the wise men do not return, Herod, in a rage, sends his soldiers to murder all boys two-years old and younger. Babies are snatched from their mothers' arms and slaughtered in their presence by Herod's soldiers. Who should we hold accountable for this carnage?

I cannot concur with the belief of the Jewish people of Jesus' time and of some modern-day Christians and Jews that evil visited on people is the result of their or their parents' sins. What sins could babies commit worthy of death? And what sins could these common people commit to justify the butchering of their babies?

A God of love would never authorize such horror. I think the slaughter of these innocent children as in the slaughter of the six million Jews under Hitler and the 16 million Russians under Stalin tell me that evil does not come from God. God is neither the author of evil nor authorizes such evil. Evil exists apart from God.

Evil tries to ensnare us. We are just as vulnerable as Jesus. You see God's love is freely given, but it is as vulnerable as that of a newborn baby. God will not interfere with our human freedom. But God wishes us to use our freedom for good and not evil.

We who believe in the resurrection know Jesus lives today and has overcome that evil which sought to destroy Him. And like Jesus we must stand up to the evils in this world. Our omissions can be just as deadly as our commissions.

Think About It

- Who are today's Herods that committed genocide in the nineteenth and twentieth century?
- What did people and governments do about these genocides?
- Do you believe God's love is vulnerable? What makes you think so?
- How do today's power brokers influence our lives?
- Why do many people pledge their allegiance to them and/or go along with them?
- What are the power brokers' ultimate destination in life and death?

20

WHY DOES GOD ALLOW EVIL TO EXIST?

BECAUSE OF OUR HUMAN LIMITATIONS, God can only be partially known. And only that which God wishes to reveal to us. Christians and Jews believe God lacks physicality and is an eternal spirit or force and creator of all that exists both visible and invisible. God has no beginning and no end. God is beyond the physical universe yet somehow present to us. God is all knowing and from whom we cannot hide. God rules the universe yet places limitations on Godself so that we may have the freedom to accept or reject God's sovereignty and to work out our own salvation. Nothing is programmed and nothing is predetermined by God. Instead, God grants us self-determination and input into the way our universe is managed be it according to God's moral order, grasping possessiveness, power grabs, and/or environmental destruction.

Christians and Jews believe God is like a loving parent. God is good and desires us to be good. Because of God's love for us, God desires a personal relationship with us but will not force us into that relationship even though God wants to occupy a place in our hearts.

Unfortunately, humanity often has ideas and feelings of its

own. We can be disobedient and listen to the calling of evil forces who suggest that we can become like God thereby causing our separation from God.

Some vulnerable, insecure, defeated and/or depressed people in troubled times seek refuge with whomever gives them a sense of security. Cult leaders take advantage of situations like these. Some leaders even claim to be God's chosen or even Jesus incarnate. Cult leaders demand followers turn over all their possessions to them. They spy upon their followers by electronically monitoring them. Often communication with other cult members is not allowed.

Rejection and intimidation are also powerful evil forces. Recently I read Jenna Miscavige Hill's book *Beyond Belief: My Secret Life Inside Scientology and My Harrowing Escape.* Jenna was raised inside this cult and is the niece of the ecclesiastical and business leader of Scientology, David Miscavige. Because of that relationship, she was not treated as harshly as the other children who were separated and abandoned by their parents who were required to be out in the world recruiting new members and promoting Scientology.

These cult children are under constant surveillance and forced into grueling work schedules, frequent psychological interrogations, coerced confessions, brain washing, harsh punishments, crowded living conditions, unreasonable restrictions, and infrequent and monitored communication with their parents. Jenna escaped this cult in 2005. She writes:

> The problem is that Scientology is a system that makes it nearly impossible for you to think for yourself. People like my uncle are enablers who create an environment of fear that discourages independent thought.

Jenna is spiritually scarred possibly for life. But she is now an independent thinker and free.

People searching and looking for answers to eternal questions unfortunately often follow the herd and fall prey to religious hucksters and what they offer if and when the vulnerable are allowed to join the cult and pay their dues. These hucksters enrich themselves on the backs of others.

We who struggle with the question of evil and the chaos it causes wonder why a good God allows evil to exist. Could it not be caused by the absence of God in people's hearts? Could it not be that God wants us to rise up and do our part just as young people across the United States are demanding there be equality and justice for all?

Should we allow the lords of chaos and evil dominate our institutions and beliefs regarding private ownership, equality, discrimination, ecological destruction, distorted religious beliefs, and businesses?

Our time and space on earth is transitory. What we do or fail to do in our lives will determine our immortal existence with God or in separation from God. Divine justice will be our reward.

Think About It

- Why do you think God allows evil to exist?
- What are your thoughts about evil and those afflicted by it?
- What role should you play regarding evil?
- What are your thoughts about cults?

21

REJECTION

I've learned that people will forget what you said,
People will forget what you did.
But people will never forget how you made them feel.
You may not control all the events that happen to you,
But you can decide not to be reduced by them.
—Maya Angelou

IN 1875 TCHAIKOVSKY first played his new Piano Concerto in B
Flat Minor for Nicholas Grigoryevich Rubinstein. Nicholas was
the founder in 1863 of the Moscow Conservatory. He was also its
director as well as the brother of Anton Rubinstein, who was a
virtuoso pianist and composer. So in 1875, Nicholas was the most
important music impresario in Russia. He was a man at the height
of his career and influence. Tchaikovsky, on the other hand, was
just coming into his own. In a letter to a friend, he wrote about an
interview he had with this influential leader of 19th Century
Russian musical life.

Tchaikovsky writes:

I performed the first movement of my new concerto. Rubinstein never opened his mouth. His silence was thunderous. I found strength to play the rest of the concerto. More silence. Well?

Then a stream poured from Rubinstein's mouth. His speech was suave at first. Then his speech gathered force and finally broke out with violence. He said my concerto was without value and wholly unperformable. He said my work was so fragmentary, disconnected and poorly composed that it could not be salvaged. The composition was bad, trivial and vulgar. He even accused me of filching from others. Then Rubenstein said perhaps only one or two pages were worth saving; the rest must be destroyed and completely recomposed.

A disinterested witness to this scene could have concluded only that I was an untalented idiot, a hack with no knowledge of composition who had the temerity to submit his rubbish to a great man. Rubinstein then said that if I alter the composition as he demanded, he'd perform it at a concert. I answered, 'I will not change one single note. And I will publish the work exactly as it is.

Although Tchaikovsky could not possibly know it at the time, he was incredibly right and Rubenstein was incredibly wrong. Tchaikovsky's concerto was published. It is one of the most popular concertos in piano literature. His fame increased so much so that in 1891, he played his concerto at the grand opening of Carnegie Hall.

Eleanor Roosevelt once said that no one can make you feel inferior without your consent. Why then do we possess feelings of inferiority and rejection?

Part of the problem may be that we live in a world of the seen and the unseen. We believe certain truths and disbelieve other truths. Based on past experiences, we project onto current events either our wish projections and longings or our negativity which causes us to believe that something is hopeless and therefore give up. With negative thinking, some of us are licked before we even confront the challenging obstacles before us.

A person's body can absorb a lot of punishment such as unrelieved thirst, unwise diet, sleepless nights, the emergency amputation of a limb without anesthetics, and/or years of back-breaking toil.

A person's mind can work without let up for days. The mind can stretch to receive and store new truths, cope with inconsistencies and contradictions, and recall more and more information.

The human heart can absorb shock, hover on the brink of despair and recover, endure loss, and bear up under the collapse of long-held dreams.

We are fearfully and wonderfully made. And yet there is one blow to which human kind is vulnerable. This is the blow that can erase a smile, buckle the knees, stoop the shoulders, snap the mind, and even break the heart. The hardest blow of all is to be rejected.

Rejection comes in a variety of forms and faces, and it can be real or imagined.

There is for instance such a thing as vocational rejection such as when a person is laid off and curtly told that his skill has become obsolete or he is no longer needed in the work place.

It is possible for one generation to reject another as when children shelve their aging parents or when parents write off all of the teen-age culture with a withering scorn.

There are tremendous feelings of rejection felt by those who are involved in a marital dispute. Husbands and wives look to something wrong in themselves, in each other, and/or to changed circumstances and commitments and/or a good dose of reality.

There can also be social rejection which is a subtle form of a caste system where people are judged and separated according to race, ethnic group, religion, education, profession, and wealth.

And there can be the rejection of self as when a person quits on himself. He grows to hate his or her own flesh and becomes a candidate for severe depression and/or suicide.

Rejection is perhaps one of the cruelest forms of social behavior. Rejection can poison our thinking and make us ill. Rejection can also send us on a furious task of trying to make ourselves acceptable to those who reject us. Nothing is more pitiable than to see people do anything asked of them so as to be accepted by some group, cult, political party, etc.

Rejection usually touches off a chain reaction that starts with self-pity and moves on to bitterness, and finally hardens into thoughts of vengeance.

It is a soul shattering experience to come upon the words "Keep Out" and know that they are meant for you. You are not wanted in this neighborhood, this organization, this job!

Rarely do people gain the acceptance they desire and need. Those rejecting them have set up arbitrary standards which are impossible for them to achieve. They can be as simple as ethnic backgrounds, hair and eye color, skin color, height and weight, and/or as complicated as education, social class and prescribed religious beliefs.

Jesus shows us an important way to handle rejection and acceptance when he prepares his disciples for rejection. In Mark 6:7-13, He tells them to focus their energies on their mission. Their mission is what counts. The disciples are Jesus' messengers. Whether they are accepted or rejected by people is the people's responsibility and not the disciples'.

The disciples are to follow Jesus' instructions. They are to proclaim the coming of the Kingdom of God, of the need for repentance and belief in the good news from God known as the gospel. In God's name they are to cast out demons, anoint and heal the sick.

This mission is similar to the mission entrusted to the church today. These practices reflect the practices of the early church. Mark pictures the disciples as flawed men similar to you and me.

Jesus does not wait for full understanding or admirable discipleship. He sends them out into the mission field as flawed men.
Their mission is a communal one. There is no single charismatic
personality around whom people are to flock. They go in pairs
because two witnesses are required in order to guarantee the truth
of what they say. They are not to tarry trying to win over those
who reject them. In time, they will grow in their discipleship by
doing and by being on the job.

The predicament of people's insensitivity to their own needs
and to the forces of evil around them is there inability to recognize evil incarnate in various individuals who have sold their
souls to the devil for success in life. Remember that before Jesus
begins his ministry he is tempted in the wilderness by the Devil
who says to him:

> "To you I will give their (kingdoms of the world) glory and all
> this authority; for it has been given over to me, and I give it to
> anyone I please. If you then, will worship me, it will all be
> yours."
>
> Jesus answered him, "It is written, 'Worship the Lord your
> God, and serve only him.'" (Luke 4:6-8)

Evil people have a destructive impact on our spiritual health
and lives. They function to divide what God has put together.
What we need to learn is how to keep them from infecting us and
others. The disciples, being flawed men, could not cast out the
evil in others by themselves. Healing and cleansing are the work
of God, but Christians can be used as God's helping instruments
in the world.

Disease, in biblical terminology, literally means "not at ease."
Disease is disharmony, disturbance, dysfunction, and disunity of
the parts of the whole.

Healing means restoration of the unity of the body, the mind,
and the spirit. The disease which seems bodily may be mental at

root. The disease which seems mental may be spiritual. The disease which seems individual may be social at the same time. The human spirit needs to be united with the divine Spirit for wholeness and health to be restored.

The interrelationship between bodily, mental, and spiritual diseases was fully understood by Jesus. Even today, we do not fully understand it. When Jesus tells his disciples to "Cure the sick, raise the dead, cleanse the lepers, cast out demons" (Matthew 10:8), He is really giving only one command. Sometimes the only way to heal is to cast out a demon or a whole host of them.

The predicament of people's insensitivity to their own needs and to the forces of evil around them is further complicated by the fact that today we misinterpret the meaning of demons. Demons are not little devils as depicted in medieval art. **"Demons" is the name given for unseen destructive forces that impact our spiritual health and lives**. These malevolent forces exist and function to divide what God has put together. What we need to learn is how to cast them out of ourselves and others. For example, the demons of resentment, revenge, drug and alcohol addiction, lust, greed, jealousy, narcissism, power, etc. can keep us from getting well spiritually, emotionally, psychologically, and physically.

Resentment is internalized anger. If we have resentment for a short time, after something unjust or unfair happens to us or a loved one that is natural. But, if we cling to resentment for months or years, we do serious damage to our health. Division within ourselves sets in.

Revenge is another demon of immeasurable power. It takes possession of us, runs us, drives us, and controls us. We protest: "I have a right to revenge. Look at what he has done to me." Revenge gets a foothold, encourages us to hold onto it; it grows in stature and control. Revenge begins to take possession of our lives and eventually says "You are mine; you belong to me."

If you are still not sure of the reality of demons, ask an alcoholic how his or her condition began, or how difficult it is to overcome. Or ask someone who is trying to recover from the power of drug addiction about the battles which go on in the human soul. A person who has not been able to whip the addiction has said: "I do not know why I did it again. I do not know what made me do it. I felt out of control as if there were another me fighting what I want to do." Division sets in. Wholeness does not exist.

That is why Jesus orders His disciples to have the people repent, believe the good news, cast out demons, anoint and heal the sick. We cannot do it alone. The medical profession can do the obvious and what is necessary physically and possibly psychologically. Spiritual healing needs to come from God. It will only come to those who are receptive to God. Christians are called to reach out with compassion to the sick, to touch them, and to love them as God's children. No societal differentiation should be made. We are to be God's wounded healers.

Jesus sent His disciples on their mission with no special equipment to be wounded healers as are we. The baggage of life is to be left behind. We are to travel lightly unencumbered by material things. We are to take only that which is necessary for the journey and no more.

Jesus tells us to be spiritually ready for rejection. He experienced it. He was despised and rejected by many people. He was a man of sorrows and acquainted with grief. He was unwanted by the religious authorities, by the government, and by society. He had no place to lay his head. And he died abandoned on a cross, suspended between Heaven and earth, as if neither wanted Him.

Jesus is calling us to share His life, to share His work, pain, and grief. He did not indulge in self-pity. He did not become embittered or stoop to vengeance. He prayed for those who did him in. Such prayers are as redemptive for the one who prays as they are for the persons prayed for.

Jesus' experience with rejection illustrates that rejection oftentimes is the result of an inadequacy within the institutions or persons doing the rejecting. There may be nothing wrong with you. The problem may reside in the other person or institutions such as in Tchaikovsky case.

The Christian faith has something else to say on the subject of rejection. No matter what the circumstances are that cause others to reject you, know that ultimately you are never alone. God loves you and accepts you with a love that will never fail.

For example, the Prodigal Son returns home expecting to be rejected as a son. Instead he finds his father accepting him. The father in this parable represents God. God loves us. We can hear that statement a thousand times without understanding it. But when we reach that point where we suffer the unspeakable pain of rejection, recall these words. God loves us! God accepts us as we are. Our striving should be only to accept God's acceptance of us.

As obedient followers of Jesus, we need to deal with people as they are, with the clean and the unclean, the polite and the rude, the solid citizens and those on the fringes of society. This means that even the most gifted disciple must expect failure as well as success, frustration as well as satisfaction, rejection as well as acceptance. If the increase is the Lord's, our task is to ensure that we have done our very best. Then we will neither be puffed up over our achievement nor guilt-ridden over our failure.

Shaking the dust from our feet is a symbolic act and witness to those who refuse to receive or listen to God's disciples who are empowered by God. Rejection by others should not dominate our lives. We need to move on and go forward. God has a purpose and mission for us. Find out what it is for you. Direct your energies towards that mission. Let all your strivings be to God's glory and in response to God's love.

Think About It

- Have you ever felt rejected? How did you react to it?
- Have you sought revenge for something bad done to you? What was the outcome?
- Do you belong to any club or organization that rejects people based on whom they are? What can you or should you do about this form of rejection?
- Do you have a better definition for demons? If so, what is it?
- How can you find peace with yourself when you are rejected?

WHY THE SLAUGHTER

A MAN SITS in front of his dressing table staring at himself in the mirror. His face is the picture of comedy with its big, empty eyes and wide, open-mouth grin. He rises, walks to his door, and enters a long corridor. He opens a door to a room filled with people wearing the mask of comedy. They are all enjoying themselves. He fits in easily with them.

In time, the man returns to his dressing table, tears off the face of comedy and puts on the face of tragedy with its downward grimace. He leaves his room and enters a room filled with people who are wearing the mask of tragedy. They are all in mourning. The man blends in well with them.

After a while the man returns to his dressing table, pulls off his mask, and to his horror discovers he has no face. His face is a blank. He puts back on his masks of comedy and then tragedy. Both will no longer fit. He cannot stand to look at himself. He rushes out into the corridor wearing a blank face and enters a third room. This room is filled with beautiful people, one more striking than the other. These people are dumbstruck by his appearance. Then they begin to draw in his face as they think it ought to look.

The man cannot stand the way they are trying to make his face conform to theirs. He rushes from the room, returns to his dressing table and wipes off his beautiful face. He opens his closet, finds a mask with the face of Jesus on it, and puts it on.

He rejoins the happy people. They cannot stand the way he smiles. When they cannot convert him to their open-mouthed, eerie grins, they attack him. He runs from the room and seeks shelter amongst the mourners. The same thing happens to him there. The mourners do not like his serenity. The man runs from his pursuers into the beautiful people's room. They find him unattractive and attack him.

He runs into the hall. There is no escape. He is savagely beaten to death. The faces of comedy, tragedy, and the beautiful people remain the same. They show no expression and no emotion. Someone then reaches down and tears off the dead man's mask of Jesus. But their bodies recoil in horror when they see the face of Jesus beneath the mask. Then the dead man rises and walks away. The people silently return to their separate rooms. Then another man goes and sits in front of the dressing table mirror.

This story, *Masks*, by John Aurelio is trying to tell us something.

1. Who is this masked man? It is hard to say. My guess is that he was a follower of Jesus who rejects all three life styles represented by comedy, tragedy, and the beautiful people.
2. Their attack on the man suggests people do not wish to have their illusions shattered by a prophet in their midst which reveals the darkness and shallowness of their lives. They do not wish to have their ideas or posturing challenged by anybody, especially Jesus or a disciple of Jesus.

3. Conformity dictates the acceptable behavior for each group. Their masks conceal who they really are.
4. This man leaves himself open to either their acceptance or rejection of him if he does not conform. Such openness is called vulnerability. Vulnerable people can be easily criticized, attacked, and destroyed. Jesus was vulnerable from the very beginning of His Life.

History has shown us that there is something about the real Jesus that unsettles most people and their schemes for living. Unless they can make Jesus into the manageable image they want Him to be cast, they will act as the Grand Inquisitor and stamp out and destroy all other images Jesus might project.

One dominant image people project onto Jesus is that of triumphalism and not one of vulnerability. They make Jesus into their own image and then claim His power and authority. They never mention Jesus' vulnerability. They justify their actions in the name of Jesus by claiming that Jesus authorizes their claims. All we need do is witness such things as Christian justification for slavery, oppression of minorities, and the slaughter of Jews and Native Americans.

Jesus comes into the world to bring us into a right relationship with God. He comes as a baby, totally vulnerable to the freedom God has given people to do either good or evil. Let's face it, we all participate in both good and evil. But too often we allow evil to exist because it does not directly affect us. When it does, it is often too late to reverse the course evil is taking without a terrible cost in lives and human suffering.

Vaulting ambition and drive for power is at the root of most evil in this world. The Herods, Neros, Caligulas, Hitlers, Stalins, Ceausescus, Putins, Kim Jong-un, Xi Jinping, Alexander Lukashenko, Basher al-Assad, ISIS and Taliban leaders, etc. will stop at nothing to claim controlling power over the populations they dominate. Their secret police and armies carry out their wicked, evil orders.

Herod's solders were no different. He was half Jew and half Idumaen. He had turned against the Jewish people and cooperated with the Roman's conquest of Palestine. As a reward he was made governor in 47 BCE. He called himself Herod the Great. He was the only ruler of Palestine who ever succeeded in keeping the peace and in bringing disorder into order. He even built the Jerusalem temple. In difficult times, he was generous. He remitted people's taxes to make things easier for them. And in the famine of 25 BCE, he melted down his gold plate to buy food for his people.

Herod's terrible flaw was suspicion. If he suspected anyone as a rival to his power, that person would be killed. He murdered members of the Sanhedrin, court officers, his wife, her mother, and two sons. Jesus would be no exception. There were perhaps 20 or 30 babies slaughtered in Bethlehem by Herod's solders in his attempt to annihilate baby Jesus.

I believe God is neither the author of evil nor authorizes such evil. Similar to Adam and Eve, God gives us our freedom to choose between good and evil. Evil exists apart from God. Evil is found in the halls of today's Herod's and in those three rooms of conformity our masked friend visited. Evil gained control over them. It will not be destroyed until they accept God's love and turn forever away from evil and the price evil exacts.

In the meantime, evil will continue to exist. Evil will try to ensnare us. We are just as vulnerable as Jesus, and like Jesus, are expected by God to use our freedom for good and not for evil.

Our spiritual road in life stretches before us. Jesus calls us to Himself. Do we have the courage to seek Him and live the selfless life Jesus wishes us to live?

Think About It

- What holds people from accepting Jesus' invitation to live as one of His followers?
- Why did the three groups of people attack the masked man?
- What are your thoughts on people who make Jesus into their own image and claim His power an authority?
- What are your thoughts on Christian justification on slavery, oppression of minorities, and slaughter of Jews, Native Americans, and other minorities?

23

A CALL TO ACTION

HAPPENINGS IN TODAY'S world distresses most people and me. Yet some of my friends do not even want to stay informed. They figure what will be will be, and they will deal with it when it happens. Elie Wiesel, a Holocaust survivor, believed the worst sin anyone can commit is to be silent in the face of evil. When he accepted the award for the Nobel Peace Prize on December 10, 1986, he said the following in his acceptance speech.

> We must always take sides. Neutrality helps the oppressor, never the victim. Silence encourages the tormentor, never the tormented. Sometimes we must interfere. When human lives are endangered, when human dignity is in jeopardy, national borders and sensitivities become irrelevant. Wherever men or women are persecuted because of their race, religion, or political views, that place must—at that moment—become the center of the Universe.

History is full of people, mostly men, who sought power and economic advantage over the lives of others through predatory practices. In the United States, the late Martin Luther King, Jr.,

John Lewis, and Elijah Cummings are three shining examples from a persecuted minority who challenged all predatory and unjust practices against their race and other under-represented and voiceless minorities. Unafraid, they rose up and shined a bright light for people to follow and to stand firm against the injustices practiced against all of them. Their crusade continues with the Black Lives Matters protests.

I pray that people of conscience will also rise up and do the same against racism and genocidal practices against the Kurds in Syria/Turkey, Myanmar Rohingya Muslims, Yazidis, displaced Syrians, and the Uyghur Muslims in China. Persecuted minorities need the United States and the world's protection against all predators, not withdrawal, silence, and the giving of green lights to the predators. We should not be pulled into darkness.

This holds true for evil cartels in countries such as Mexico and Central America where protection money must be paid to them by innocent civilians if they wish to stay alive and keep their children from being drafted into the cartels to be foot soldiers and sex slaves. We need to willingly leave our comfort zone to aid and assist vulnerable people who are preyed upon in this world. It is my hope that young people like Greta Thunberg will start a movement that challenges people of all ages to rise up with them and shine a light on predators and resist their evil practices.

I pray that people will accept God's calling to protect the innocent and vulnerable. May God bless, guide and protect them and give them the courage, energy, and wisdom necessary to confront and overcome all obstacles. It is my hope that these predators and their predatory practices will be brought to justice so that good will, peace, and justice will be part of everyone's life.

Think About it

- What are your thoughts on today's genocides? What can you do about them?
- Why do you think anti-Semitism is on the rise? What can you do about it?
- What can you do about white supremacy?
- How and why have political leaders given the green light for the persecution of minorities?
- Actions and inactions have consequences. How can we call ourselves God's people when we turn a blind eye on unbridled evil?
- What can you do to help the persecuted?

24

JOHN THE BAPTIST, JESUS' BAPTISM AND TEMPTATIONS

WE DON'T KNOW anything about John the Baptist's early life. His parents probably died of old age when he was very young. What we do know is that he lived in the wilderness away from cities and towns. Many scholars consider John to be the last of the Old Testament prophets.

In 28 CE,

> John the baptizer appeared in the wilderness, proclaiming a
> baptism of repentance for the forgiveness of sins. And people
> from the whole Judean countryside and all the people of
> Jerusalem were going out to him, and were baptized by him in
> the river Jordan, confessing their sins. (Mark 1:4-5)

John's preaching undermines the religious establishment's hold on the people. Jewish people did not believe it necessary to be baptized for the forgiveness of sins since they believed their sacrifices to God of an unblemished animal removed their sins. They believed their sins were transferred to the poor animal; and with its death, their sins were removed. Also, Jews did not believe in baptism. Converts to Judaism known as proselytes were the only ones baptized.

So, what is John's message? He tells the people to:

- *Repent.* Repentance is *sorrow* for wrongs we have committed. It is an *admission of fault.* It is an *attempt* to right the wrongs committed by us. True repentance brings us into a new and better relationship with God.
- *Turn away from your sins.*
- *Be baptized* as a sign of your desire to live a new life. Then God will forgive you.

John's baptism is a baptism with water. He says that Jesus' baptism will be with the Holy Spirit and fire. John uses an agricultural image of farmers separating the wheat from the useless chaff. The wheat will be saved, and the chaff will be burned. In essence, John is saying that when Jesus comes people will have to make a decision. They can either respond to Jesus' invitation which will lead to their salvation. Or they can reject His invitation which will lead to their condemnation.

Out of this throng of people in the wilderness, Jesus steps forward to be baptized by John who instinctively recognizes his unworthiness to baptize Jesus. But Jesus insists that John baptize Him and so he did.

> And just as he was coming out of the water, he saw the heavens torn apart and the Spirit descending like a dove upon him. And a voice came from heaven, 'you are my Son, the Beloved; with you I am well pleased.' And the Spirit immediately drove him out into the wilderness. (Mark 1:10-12)

I often wonder why Jesus waited so long to begin his ministry. It could have been that Mary told him about how she was overshadowed by the Holy Spirit thereby making her pregnant with Him without any sexual intercourse. Also, the knowledge of Herod's slaughter of boys under two years old in an attempt to kill Him caused Jesus to keep a very low profile until he was ready for ministry. It could be that He used this time to grow in wisdom in the ways of God.

Upon Jesus' baptism, He has a vision that reaffirms his mission and ministry. According to what Jesus told His disciples about this moment in time, no one else experienced or saw what Jesus experienced when He was baptized. Yet John 1:32-34 tells a different version of this event and how John the Baptist witnessed the descent of the Holy Spirit upon Jesus.

With the baptism of Jesus, John the Baptist knows that his mission is over. He does not hang on to his position as the forerunner of the Messiah. Jesus is now ready to begin his ministry. The old passes away. John the Baptist is taken prisoner by Herod's soldiers and is eventually beheaded.

After His baptism, Jesus is led away by the Spirit into the wilderness, to be tempted by the devil. Here Jesus will test His baptismal vision and His future course of action. In the wilderness, there is a struggle for survival; life and death issues stand out in all their starkness. The trappings of society do not hide them. The meaning of life takes on new meaning in this environment. As Jesus must have done, we need to ask ourselves if we are to live only for the sake of survival, as the animals do. Or are we to live in such a way that we fulfill God's purposes for us.

It is believed that Jesus purposefully went into the wilderness to think and pray about what shape his ministry would take. Jesus probably fasted for 40 days which means for a long time. This fasting meant that he probably took water and little else. He could not have survived without water, because He would become dehydrated. Jesus was just as human as we are.

Gospel writers used *the literary device of an imaginary debate* by Jesus with the forces of evil represented by the devil or evil personified. Jesus' debate with the devil also outlines temptations we have and decisions we must make in life.

For a temptation to be real, there must be the possibility of choice. By rejecting each temptation made by the devil, Jesus made a conscious choice as to the shape His ministry will take.

Let us examine Jesus' three wilderness temptations by the devil. The devil is a name given to living forms of evil. Evil can come in many forms. The evil Jesus experiences could be internal as well as external.

The first temptation deals with our body. Jesus had fasted for a long time. His hunger is real. First, Jesus' identity is questioned with the word "If." Jesus makes no reply to

"If" you are God's son, order this stone to turn into bread. (Luke 4:3)

Jesus' answer to the rest of the devil's question was that people cannot live on bread alone. An enduring belief in God must survive hunger, sickness, and maltreatment. A bread and butter relationship would only lead to a master-slave relationship. Obedience to God then would not be out of love but rather a fear of losing one's meal ticket. Jesus rejected the idea of converting the world to God's ways through a master/slave, bread and butter relationship. Also, Jesus rejects materialism. Material things, including food, will not bring people closer to God. In fact, Jesus believes that possessions often separate people from God.

Then the devil led him up and showed him in an instant all the kingdoms of the world. And the devil said to him, 'To you I will give their glory and all this authority; for it has been given over to me, and I give it to anyone I please. If you, then, will worship me, it will all be yours.' (Luke 4:6-7)

The devil is now claiming to be in charge of all the universe.

He is offering Jesus the world on the condition that Jesus worship the devil. Many Jews believed that the Messiah would be a warrior king similar to David who would drive out the Romans and restore Israel to its former glory. What the Jews had forgotten is that the consequences of David's and Solomon's unlimited power sowed the seeds of destruction for their kingdom. Jesus would not seek desirable ends by unworthy means. Idolatrous worship of power and earthly things would not be part of Jesus' ministry. Through Jesus' love and sacrifice, He would try to win people's hearts and souls. Jesus' response to this temptation was we are to worship the Lord our God and serve only God.

> Then the devil took him to Jerusalem, and placed him on the pinnacle of the temple, saying to him, 'If you are the Son of God, throw yourself down from here, for it is written, He will command his angels concerning you, to protect you and On their hands they will bear you up, so that you will not dash your foot against a stone.' (Luke 4:9-11)

Spectacles do not create an enduring faith. Jesus told the devil not to put the Lord your God to the test. Jesus wanted people to respond to His message and to whom He is and nothing else.

Jesus wants to redeem the world. He wants to conquer the evil that exists in people's hearts and minds. The contest is between the material and the spiritual world. Love of the material world separates people from God. Love of God brings people into communion with God.

Jesus will not admit evil into His spiritual world by succumbing to the temptations of the devil. Nevertheless, external evil overpowers Jesus and brings Him to the cross.

The story of Jesus' temptations is our story. We are all vulnerable and vacillate when it comes to our bodily needs, pride, and worship of power. It is important to remember Jesus' admonition to His disciples. He says:

If any man would come after me, let him deny himself and take up his cross and follow me. For whoever would save his life will lose it, and whoever loses his life for my sake will find it. For what will it profit a man, if he gains the whole world and forfeits his life? (Matthew 16:24-26)

If we decide to follow Jesus and His example, we need to remember that the world crucified Him once and would do so again. It is difficult to live as a Christian and to resist these three temptations in our life's journey. Jesus' Great Invitation to us will help us through the uncertain days and years ahead. He says:

Come to me, all who labor and are heavy laden, and I will give you rest. Take my yoke upon you and learn from me; for I am gentle and lowly in heart, and you will find rest for your soul. For my yoke is easy, and my burden is light. (Luke 4:9-11)

Think About It

- Why do you think Jesus waited to begin His ministry?
- Why do you think Jews sought John the Baptist's baptism?
- What are your thoughts on repentance?
- Do you think Jesus' three temptations in the wilderness actually occurred or were they an internal struggle within Jesus as to his future ministry?
- What does Jesus mean when He says that people cannot live a good life on bread alone?
- Name world leaders that you think have given their soul to the devil and with what success? Who benefits?
- Why did the devil question Jesus as to His being God's Son?

25

JESUS BEGINS HIS MINISTRY

JESUS HAS BEEN BAPTIZED and tested for 40 days and nights in the wilderness. He returns to civilization and begins His ministry by preaching the gospel. The "gospel" means the good news from God. Jesus says:

> The time is fulfilled, and the Kingdom of God is at hand; repent and believe in the gospel. (Mark 1:15)

According to Mark, this one sentence contains in a nutshell the message and purpose of Jesus' ministry.

So, what is the Kingdom of God? There are many interpretations, too many to enumerate here. For Jesus, it meant the establishment of God's rule on earth. It is a spiritual reality and a work in progress in which we can participate. Admission to the Kingdom of God requires that we repent and believe in the gospel. We have to make a decision as to our loyalty to God and whether we will let God reign in our hearts and be God's instrument of peace or go on our own self-asserted way.

When Jesus returns to Nazareth, His healing ministry is well known. Everyone goes to the synagogue to hear him speak. It was common practice to let those who were able to select a reading from the prophets and deliver a sermon on it. Jesus reads from Isaiah 61:1-2 and 58:6 regarding the exiles' day of deliverance which also expresses the pattern Jesus' ministry will take. He makes a royal proclamation of amnesty and release. Jesus announces to Israel that God reigns and God's reign is to be exercised through pardon, healing, and liberation.

- Jesus announces that a new age begins with Him. He has harsh criticism for those in power. His message is for the poor and the captives such as the bonded slaves and the oppressed.
- His message is also a warning of judgment to those who oppress or fail to help others.
- He announces who He is and what He intends to do while on earth when He reads Isaiah's prophecy in the Nazareth synagogue.

- The Spirit of the Lord is upon me, because he has anointed me to bring good news to the poor.
- He has sent me to proclaim release to the captives and recovery of sight to the blind,
- To let the oppressed go free,
- To proclaim the year of the Lord's favor.

And he rolled up the scroll, gave it back to the attendant, and sat down. The eyes of all in the synagogue were fixed on him. Then he began to say to them, "Today this scripture has been fulfilled in your hearing." (Luke 4:18-21)

At first all speak well of him. Then their admiration turns to hostility and injured pride. How can the carpenter's son be the Son of God, and why doesn't He perform His miracles in Nazareth? The people's anger turns ugly, and they try to kill

Jesus. Their actions are a foretaste of the treatment his countrymen will heap upon Him.

Jesus walks unafraid through the angry crowd. No one touches Him. He leaves town and goes to Capernaum. There is no reason to stay where He is not wanted.

The Kingdom of God begins in our lives when we accept Jesus as our Lord and master, when we commit our lives to Him, follow Him, and are obedient to Him.

Jesus announces the kingdom's coming upon us. For Jesus, this means the immediate future. It will be Jesus' authoritative words and deeds that will open the Kingdom of God for us. Jesus makes an appeal to us. He wants us to repent and believe in the gospel. True, we must feel sorry for our sins. But repentance would be of little value without belief in the good news from God.

In Galilee, Jesus was present in the flesh. For us, Jesus is present to us through the Holy Spirit, the gospels, and in other believers who carry on His work. Wherever the gospel is faithfully preached and studied, the Kingdom of God draws near. Those who hear, believe, and carry out God's will are the ones who become a part of the Kingdom of God.

Two themes dominate the gospel of Mark. There is the Messianic secrecy theme in the first half of the gospel. This secrecy theme lessens and disappears as it becomes clear who Jesus is and what is the nature of messiahship. The second theme is the incomprehension of His disciples. Their apparent dull wittedness spans the entire gospel and does not disappear until after the cross. Only from the perspective of the cross do they understand what it means to be the Messiah. From the cross, all becomes perceptible for those who have ears to hear and eyes to see.

Jesus' disciples and the Christian readers of Mark's gospel are considered insiders and privy to Jesus' parabolic explanations (See Mark 4). We are in some manner present among the hearers.

Jesus tells us that it is not God who blinds people to the faith and the message being sent to the people. Their blindness is their own fault. They are like the seed that is scattered along the path. They are the no-growth people. They may hear Jesus, but they do not want to respond to Him. They are the hardened, spiritually dead people whose wills refuse to let the Word of God penetrate through to their consciousness.

The next group, the shallow growth people receive with joy Jesus' Word, but they do not take deep root and are intellectually without roots. They disappear in the mid-day sun.

The third group, the stunted growth people receive the word, but their seed is planted in a divided mind. There is competition between the cares of the world, riches, and other competing desires with their vision of the Kingdom of God.

The last group, the full growth people hear the Word of God and bear a bountiful harvest.

The point of the parable of the sower is that in spite of many obstacles and opposition to Jesus and His ministry there will be ultimate success for God's kingdom. It is present in Jesus, in His works and words. But for the moment, only the disciples can understand this truth and even they need to be taught. For outsiders, God's gift of revelation will remain incomprehensible. From the perspective of the cross, Jesus' disciples will reveal and will illume to all Jesus' message and true identity.

Think About It

- What are your thoughts about the Kingdom of God?
- When and where do you enter it?
- Why do some have trouble understanding Jesus' parabolic explanations?
- Why did the people in Nazareth and today reject Jesus' announcement regarding His mission?

26

ARE YOU A RELIGIOUS SKEPTIC?

MANY, many people may not be atheists but are uncertain what to believe. They are confronted with hundreds of opposing theological and atheistic options. Many would-be Christians are disillusioned and/or are repelled by ill-equipped clergy, clergy abuses, hell and damnation teachings, religious cults, ignorance, and numerous heresies. But I will not let them make me an atheist.

I question and doubt many things in life. I welcome my doubt and have come to think of it as an invitation to think critically. I have a tendency to overthink most truths. As a young person and even today, I have difficulty answering standard multiple-choice questions because the possible answers do not cover all possibilities. So, I have to choose among inadequate answers. I do much better when I can answer a question with a written response that requires my analysis. I have always had to look at all sides of an issue or belief before coming to any conclusions. My doubts and thinking challenge me to seek and discover a clearer, deeper understanding of God's role in my life and in the universe. And with God's help, my pilgrimage, my doubts, and my struggles for a clearer understanding of God may assist me in guiding other faith seekers.

I believe there is meaning and purpose to our lives and the directions they take. I think we should not overlook the wisdom of the ages. For starters, let us take another look at the Bible, the sacred scripture of the Jewish and Christian people. The Bible is a thoroughly human collection of books written over several centuries by many different authors that tell of people's experiences with God, their limited understanding of God, their relationship to God, and their commitment or lack of commitment to following God's commands and God's authority over them. Within the Jewish and Christian community, theologians, scholars, clergy, and believers all interpret these scriptures differently. So, who has the correct understanding?

I like the fact that the authors of the Book of Exodus expose Moses' disbelief and his resistance to God. Remember Moses was raised by Pharaoh's daughter and knew nothing about the God of Abraham, Isaac, and Jacob. What he knew of God may have come from his father-in-law Jethro. Moses' excuses could be our excuses. His attraction to the burning bush on Mt. Sinai could be our attraction. Why wasn't the bush consumed? The laws of nature tell us that it should be. Some say the fire symbolizes the presence of God.

In the back of Moses' mind, I think he fears the Israelites and that he will suffer even more at the hands of Pharaoh if he follows God's orders. And he is right? After all, Pharaoh believes he is god. Pharaoh represents all the false gods and despots of every generation, and how dare the Israelite's challenge his godhead free of any consequences.

Moses reluctantly takes leave of Jethro and with his family returns to Egypt. His greatest fears initially take place; i.e., the Israelite leaders' resist Moses' instructions from God, more repressions by Pharaoh occur, ten plagues visit the land, and the death of the first born. At the end of these events, the Israelites leave Egypt, wander in the wilderness for a generation, form themselves into a faith community, make a covenant with God, and then enter the Promised Land.

Fast forward to Jesus in the Nazareth synagogue with His reading from Isaiah 61. I repeat here what Jesus says:

> The Spirit of the Lord is upon me, because he has anointed me to bring good news to the poor. He has sent me to proclaim release to the captives and recovery of sight to the blind, to let the oppressed go free, to proclaim the year of the Lord's favor. (Luke 4:18-19)

So, what is Jesus saying here? I believe Jesus wants to redeem the world. He wants to conquer the evil that exists in peoples' hearts and minds. He wants people to see beyond the material world and bring people closer to God. He wants to remove the spiritual blinders from our eyes that hold us captive.

Only after Jesus' resurrection did Jesus' disciples begin to understand what Jesus was all about. Before Jesus' death, His disciples had visions of an earthly Messiah who would lead Israel victoriously over the oppressors of their day. They did not expect a dead Messiah or a resurrected Messiah or the gift of the Holy Spirit. Eventually they came to realize that Jesus is the clearest revelation we have of God, that Jesus is from God, and that God exists in and beyond this universe and our understanding.

I believe we human beings are limited by our humanity. No one person knows and understands everything, especially about God.

The seductions of this world are very attractive. If they were unappealing, no one would be attracted to them. I think we can take a lesson from Homer's *Odyssey*. Odysseus is trying to get home after the Trojan War. Circe tells him of the dangers he will face while he tries to sail past the island on which the Sirens live. She tells him and his men to plug their ears with beeswax so they cannot hear the Sirens beckoning calls. Ah, but Odysseus wants to hear what they have to say. So, he plugs the ears of his crew, and he has his crew bind him to the mast so that he cannot break free. As they sail past the Siren's island, the Sirens promise to reveal to Odysseus the future. Odysseus wants to hear more and tries to release himself. His men bind him even tighter. They manage to past the Sirens' island and escape their expected shipwreck and death. So, too, I suggest we all should beware of the fortune tellers, religious hucksters, and Sirens in life as we travel through life to our final destination.

I believe God speaks to us and tests us in many ways. If we are open to God, God will be present to us through the Holy Spirit, through other people, through events in our lives, through scripture, and music. We have reasons to doubt and reasons to believe. We need to learn to live with these tensions and let them compel us to seek a deeper understanding of the purpose for our lives as God's children.

Think of doubt as an invitation to think more critically and deeply and the start of a spiritual pilgrimage of discovery. Doubt opens a new way of looking at the world and God. Doubt causes us to examine multiple beliefs systems. Doubt makes us educate ourselves by reading some good books on the history of Christianity and the controversies surrounding many Christian beliefs. Faith is not just a mind thing. Listen to good Christian music that will stir your soul. Music is known as the language of the heart and often is more profound than just words. Be watchful. Learn from peace loving, giving, caring people who work for the welfare of needy people in the wider world. They are God's hands and voice.

Think About It

- What are your beliefs and disbeliefs about Jesus?
- How do you respond to Jesus' call today?
- Do your doubts challenge you to confront opposing and questionable answers to existential questions?

27

HOW DO YOU HANDLE WORLDLY TEMPTATIONS?

In one of Jesus' temptations in the wilderness, the devil shows Jesus all the kingdoms of the world in a moment of time. The devil offers to turn over his authority to rule the world to Jesus in return for Jesus' worship of the devil. Jesus answers him: "It is written, 'Worship the Lord your God, and serve only him.'" Jesus will not seek desirable ends by unworthy means.

Most people like to be masters of their own destiny. Jesus did not want people to grudgingly follow Him because they would feel enslaved rather than free.

Perhaps Jesus knew that part of the yeast in life is to strive, to complain, to be challenged, and then to be required to make choices that will determine an unknown future. Jesus' rejection of the devil's temptations reveals Jesus' great insight into human nature and human need. He does not surrender to the moment. He knows that human beings can be stifled if the spiritual is not in a proper balance with the physical and emotional nature of people.

Shakespeare's Macbeth is a good example of a person who capitalized on a moment in time to win for himself a kingdom. He is hailed by three witches on a heath as the future king of Scotland. Macbeth then becomes agitated in mind. He returns home. Lady Macbeth is seized with ambition for her husband and greets him by saying:

> Your letters have transported me beyond
> This ignorant present, and I feel now
> The future in an instant. (Act 1, Scene V)

She felt the future in an instant? She only imagined that she felt the future in an instant. Her future would be different from her perception of it. What did she base her future on? The prophecy of the witches? All the witches did was to hail Macbeth as king. They said nothing else. Yet the witches' prophecies set in motion grandiose ideas of power, glory, and majesty. The price tag was never predicted. The path to the throne was never outlined. Macbeth's and Lady Macbeth's future became a future of their own making that led to deception and murder.

A little later in time Duncan, the king of Scotland, pays a visit to Macbeth's castle. Lady Macbeth takes advantage of this opportunity to make Macbeth king by killing King Duncan. The cost to Lady Macbeth is sleeplessness, mental disorder, and a vain attempt to wash the blood from her hands. Finally, she commits suicide.

When Macbeth learns of his wife's suicide, he is preparing to enter his last battle. There is no time to mourn her. He is resigned to his fate. Experience has given him a different world view from the one he knew and perceived before he met the witches. Macbeth says:

> Tomorrow, and tomorrow, and tomorrow
> Creeps in this petty paced from day to day,
> To the last syllable of recorded time,
> And all our yesterdays have lighted fools
> The way to dusty death. Out, out, brief candle!
> Life's but a walking shadow, a poor player

That struts and frets his hour upon the stage
And then is heard no more. It is a tale
Told by an idiot, full of sound and fury,
Signifying nothing. (Act V, Scene V)

Macbeth sounds like the Preacher in Ecclesiastes 1. "All is vanity and a striving after wind." Macbeth heard what he imagined to be a fair prophecy. No choice was demanded of him. He acted out of his free will. Macbeth sold his precious freedom for the bondage of sin. He made his future the dismal failure it became.

Let us now return to Jesus. Did He see His future in a moment in time? I believe that Jesus knew that going against the legalistic, religious establishment of His day would lead him into trouble. But I do not believe He realized the full extent He would suffer, be humiliated, and abandoned. Jesus was betrayed, mocked, spat at, whipped with scourges, stripped of clothing, and crucified. Had He seen all this in that moment in time, I doubt His anguish, His sense of complete failure and abandonment would have been heard in His words: "My God, my God, why have you forsaken me?" (Matthew 27:46)

And what about us? Do we see our future in a moment in time or do we just imagine that we do? If we think of eternity in terms of linear time as having no beginning and no end, we are but a tiny dot along this endless line. Roy Clark who wrote the song *Yesterday When I was Young* illustrates how many of us unwittingly live our lives. You can hear this song on YouTube. Selected lyrics are as follows:

Yesterday when I was young the taste of life was sweet as rain upon my tongue. I teased at life as if it were a foolish game... A thousand dreams I dreamed and splendid things I planned I always built to last on weak and shifting sand....

There are so many songs in me that won't be sung. I feel the
bitter taste of tears upon my tongue. The time has come for me
to pay for yesterday when I was young.

In essence, this song re-echo's Pascal's belief that we turn
eternity into nothing, and nothing into eternity. Pascal believed
that our imaginations, our illusive dreams so preoccupy us and
our thinking that there is no time left to think about or prepare
our souls for eternity and our existence beyond this life. Because
many of us do not think about eternity or life after death, we
waste the present and reduce eternity in our minds to nothing. If
we are not careful, the strivings of our lives will supplant the
eternity God has planned for us.

Let us go back to Jesus' answer to the devil's offer of all the
kingdoms of the world. "You shall worship the Lord your God,
and Him only shall you serve." This quotation comes from the
Book of Deuteronomy in the context where God is testing and
humbling His people in the wilderness. Jesus' response to the
devil reveals Jesus' inner vision, a vision of the experiences of
the Israelites. Jesus picked up this vision and appropriated it for
His time and circumstances. We, too, can have a similar vision
for our lives. We know we cannot catch the wind nor alter the
direction it blows. We should not build our lives on weak and
shifting sand. But unlike the Preacher in Ecclesiastes, Christians
have learned through Jesus to affirm life, to avoid the bondage of
sin, to accept with joy the time given us and the toil which is our
lot. We seek to nourish and balance our spiritual lives with the
rest of life.

Think About It

- During Lent, Christians are supposed to take an
  inventory of their lives. Do you?

- Do you take this time to repent of your sins?
- Do you seek to repair the damage you may have caused to others and yourself?
- Do you pray for a new and better relationship with God?

28

SOME EVERYDAY SPIRITUAL CHALLENGES

IN THIS CHAPTER, I have put together several random thoughts on our everyday spiritual challenges.

The Company You Keep

In the early twentieth century, a hastily formed volunteer posse chases bank robbers on horseback. Each member has his reason for joining this posse. But one by one, each man demonstrates his integrity or lack thereof and stamina. After desertions and a shoot-out with the robbers and the recovery of the stolen money, the sheriff and a corrupt gambler are the last two men standing. Each man's destiny is tied to the money bags. The gambler plays his hand and draws his gun on the sheriff who is only doing his duty and wants to return the money to the bank depositors.

- What will be the short and long-term gains or losses in this situation?
- Who is the real winner—the gambler, the sheriff, and/or the depositors? What makes you think so?

Greed, Possessions, and Excesses

A man in the crowd asks Jesus to tell his brother to divide the family inheritance with him. Jesus' response is a warning. He says:

> Take care! Be on your guard against all kinds of greed; for one's life does not consist in the abundance of possessions. (Luke 12:15)

Jesus illustrates what he means in a parable about a rich man who had such a large harvest who planned to tear down his barns and build larger ones to house his produce. Then he could spend the rest of his life relaxing, eating, drinking, and being merry. Unfortunately, that night his life was demanded of him. (Luke 12:16-23)

There are many different ways to interpret this parable. Jesus doesn't respond directly to the man in the crowd. Instead Jesus delves into our relationship with our possessions. The overriding theme of this parable is the folly of greed and the hoarding of one's possessions.

The rich man is neither a bad man nor a good man. Why do I say that? He did not cheat or steal from anyone. He did not mistreat his workers. Yet Jesus calls him a fool. Why? Could it be that he lives solely for himself? So, what is wrong with that? What is missing in his thinking is that his and our physical lives are on loan to us. He was rich but not rich towards God. He failed to understand that the only possessions worthy of striving for are those death cannot take away. In fact, covetousness is a form of idolatry that replaces God with material things when in fact our lives should be a preparation for the life to come.

Many people are like the rich man who work hard, save their money, and plan for their retirement so that they can live independently and not be a burden to family and society.

So, let us ask ourselves what would you do if you were rich like the farmer or if you won the lottery? In 1886 Leo Tolstoy wrote a short story entitled *How Much Land Does a Man Need?* You probably know this story. It tells us about Pahom, a peasant farmer who becomes obsessed with owning more and more land. He even boasts that with enough land he would not even fear the devil himself. One day Pahom learns he can acquire from the Bakshirs for 1,000 rubles all the land he can mark off from sunup to sundown provided he returns to his starting point before the sun sets. If he doesn't get there in time, he will lose his 1,000 rubles. In his covetousness, he tries to encircle and place markers on 35 miles of land, some of which he plans to sell off in the future at a profit. About midday he realizes he has gone too far and asks himself "Will God let me live on this land?" Exhausted, Pahom tries to circle back to the starting point. He reaches it minutes before the sun sets. Then he drops dead. His servant picks up Pahom's shovel and digs a six-foot grave for him. That is all the land he needed.

Now let us look at two people in particular who take an opposite approach to life's opportunities.

- Recently, in France, a 22-year-old man named Gassama from Mali risked his life to save a four-year old boy dangling precariously on the outside railing of a fifth-floor balcony. Gassama scaled five stories of the apartment building and moved from balcony to balcony to rescue the boy. He thought nothing about his own safety. When he rescues the boy, the crowds below applauded him and dubbed him "Spider-Man". President Emmanuel Macron invited Gassama to the presidential Elysee Palace in Paris and rewarded Gassama with an offer of citizenship and a job as a firefighter.
- LeBron James, a professional basketball player for the

Los Angeles Lakers has set an example of what rightfully deployed money can do to better the lives of others. He recently helped bankroll a new public school called I Promise School for at-risk children in his hometown of Akron, Ohio. Students are given bikes, uniforms, hot meals, and the families of the students will have access to a food pantry. The inaugural class had 240 third and fourth graders. Eventually they expect to have over 1,000 students. LeBron has pledged free college tuition at the University of Akron for every student who graduates from the I Promise School.

Considering the examples I have just given, ask yourself where do you stand in relation to the rich man in Jesus' parable, Tolstoy's Phahom, Gassama, and LeBron James?

- Do you live only for yourself and your families or do you seek to help the needy?
- How does your relationship or absent a relationship with God dictate your behavior?
- Where do you place your trust for today and tomorrow?
- What do you do with your excesses beyond your basic needs of clothing, shelter, food, medical, and health care?
- Are you like the rich man morally and spiritually indifferent to other people's needs?
- These questions only you can prayerfully think about and answer.

I am personally biased regarding our treatment of refugees, displaced persons, asylum seekers, the homeless, the starving, and the poverty stricken.

I do not believe we can be morally and spiritually indifferent to today's refugees fleeing war, violence, persecutions, evil, genocide, and predatory practices within their home countries. Coming to the aid of refugees may be an inconvenience and costly. But like the rich man in today's parable, we will be held accountable.

And in this regard, we need to remember that none of us own the land and our possessions. They are on loan to us. They belong to God even though we fight over it. Also, Native Americans were here before the invasion of the white man who took much of their land.

My takeaway from this parable and our responsibility towards are neighbors comes from Jesus who said "to whom much has been given, much will be required; and from the one to whom much has been entrusted, even more will be demanded." (Luke 12:48)

The prayer of St. Francis of Assisi helps guide us on our spiritual journey. He prays:

Lord make me an instrument of your peace
Where there is hatred let me sow love
Where there is injury, pardon
Where there is doubt, faith
Where there is despair, hope
Where there is darkness, light
And where there is sadness, joy

O divine master grant that I may
Not so much seek to be consoled as to console
To be understood as to understand
To be loved as to love

For it is in giving that we receive
It is in pardoning that we are pardoned

And it's in dying that we are born to eternal life. Amen

Who Owns the Earth?

The earth is the Lord's and all that is in it, the world, and those who live in it; for he has founded it on the seas, and established it on the rivers. (Psalm 24:1-2)

If the earth is the Lord's and all that is in it, why do politicians and businesses rule the day in dialing back the Clean Air Act by continuing to pollute the air we breathe and the water we drink? Why do they allow deforestation through logging, mining, water pollution, coal-powered electric-generating plants, the impending extinction of wildlife plants, animals, and sea life, and so on? Do we not all have a very short life span on this earth to be followed by succeeding generations who also have a short life span?

Greta Thunberg, a teenage Swedish environmental activist, and millions of other like-minded people are crusading to stop everything that contributes to climate change and its impact on their future. Economics and income inequality contribute to this complicated and vicious cycle of exploitation.

Those people who profit from ravaging the environment state that the science behind our foreseeable environmental catastrophe cannot be proved. To me, that posture is similar to the naysayers who said we couldn't put a man on the moon or that the earth is round.

Personal gain created twentieth century jobs in polluting industries that lifted people out of poverty even though they were subjected to black-lung and other diseases. Therefore, people are afraid to challenge businesses and politicians who allow the degradation of our environment because of the impact it will have on their short-term economic well-being.

Greta and people like her have the backbone and determination to challenge our earthly predators who enact laws that benefit them, their bank accounts, and fleece the world's natural resources. She and others are trying to save the future of this world.

Think About It

- Do you question Greta and other climate change environmentalists? If so, why do you?
- What right and/or claim do businesses and politicians have to the land? Do they really own the land? Do you own the land? What makes you think so?
- What sacrifices are you willing to make to reduce your ecological footprint?
- How can businesses and politicians help displaced and laid-off workers?
- Should polluting industries shut down?
- Is pollution a crime against humanity? If so, what makes you think so?

What role do you think God wants us to play regarding climate change?

Separated, Trapped, and Gone

One morning as I was preparing my breakfast, I looked out of my kitchen window to see a doe and a fawn grazing on my lawn—a normal occurrence. Then out of nowhere, I noticed the doe's other fawn near my neighbors' 10-foot deer fence which stretched along my property line. At first, I thought the fawn was on my property, but then I noticed it running from one end of the fence to the other trying to find an opening to join his mother and sibling on my property. Occasionally, the fawn wandered further into my neighbor's property seeking a way out.

As the sun rose higher in the sky, the doe and fawn wondered off my property and into the woods leaving behind the trapped fawn. Then I was distracted for a few minutes fixing my breakfast. The next time I looked out my window, I never saw the trapped fawn again. Did it escape by going to the front of my neighbor's property even though it was gated? Did it die of exhaustion? Or did my neighbor shoot it with a bow and arrow? I will never know. Yet the doe and her fawn still graze on my property shortly after sunrise and shortly before sunset.

The fence, the doe, and her fawns made me think of the US border wall and barriers in other countries that harm fellow human beings by excluding them. Unfortunately, history seems to repeat itself.

Today millions of people struggle to survive senseless and harmful barriers, brutalities of war, dictators, autocrats, predators, human traffickers, slave holders, terrorists, and the like. Most vulnerable people find it necessary to escape these life-threatening conditions in their home countries. Their hope is that the international community will open their doors and allow them a safe haven until such time as peace, justice, and stability are established in their home countries so they can return and rebuild their lives there.

In the meantime, let us recognize the dignity and worth of refugees and asylum seekers and give them the respect and equal rights they deserve as God's children. And let us live out Jesus' great love commandment.

> You shall love the Lord your God with all your heart, and with all your soul, and with all your mind. This is the greatest and first commandment. And a second is like it: You shall love your neighbor as yourself. On these two commandments hang all the law and the prophets. (Matthew 22:37-40)

Think About It

- What would you do if you lived in intolerable situations as millions of people currently do?
- What rights should asylum seekers have?
- What can you do to help persecuted minorities?
- What are your thoughts about imprisonment of asylum seekers at the US border where children are separated from their parents?
- What can or should you do about these situations?

A Child's Cry

Hearing the roar of an overhead helicopter
My heart fills with sorrow.
Instinctively, I think I should seek shelter because
Images of starving and dismembered Yemeni civilians
Come to mind.

I see a child crying over his dead mother and sister.
Bombs have destroyed all surrounding buildings.
Their rubble litters the ground.

Poor child. What is your future? Will you have food to eat?
If you survive and grow to be a man,
Will you seek revenge from the destroyers?
Or will you with the help of other survivors
Be able to bring all power struggles to an end?
And will you and others be able to bring
Peace on earth and good will towards everyone?

Light and Darkness

The light shines in the darkness, and the darkness did not overcome it. (John 1:5)

A lot of people believe God doesn't exist, that God is only a fanciful projection of our minds. That is their choice. But their disbelief does not mean that God does not exist. Some Jews in hiding from the Nazis in World War II wrote on a cellar wall in Cologne the following inscription. "I believe in the sun, even when it is not shining. I believe in love, even when not feeling it. I believe in God, even when God is silent."

When John says Jesus is the *Light* of the World, he refers to the divine illumination of a person's mind and conscience. This light dispels human darkness and continues throughout time. The word *Life* refers to the function of the Holy Spirit that represents the positive aspects of life and existence. Life represents the authentic existence God wants us to have. Life and salvation are associated with light.

Darkness is symbolic of disbelief as well as total evil that cannot overcome the Word. Jesus comes into the world as a human being to have a flesh and blood relationship with us. Jesus partially reveals to us the mind of God. As the Word, Jesus brings light into our midst to dispel the darkness; but many turn their backs on His light.

The Parable of the Light Bulb

An old, tall lamp flickered occasionally when it was turned on. I paid no attention to it so long as it functioned and provided the necessary light. Then one night, while I was reading in bed, sparks ignited a fire around the light-bulb's socket. I reached to turn off the lamp's switch but realized I would burn my hands. So. I pulled the plug and the power behind the fire was extinguished.

The next day, I looked online for a replacement lamp. In my

search, I learned that lamps have maximum proscribed light-bulb wattage. Perhaps the light bulb I was using exceeded the limitations built for my bedside lamp. Perhaps my home was almost lost for violating the lamp creator's restrictions that were forgotten or ignored by me for years.

It took more than a week for the stench of the fire to dissipate.

Think About It

- Are we like a lamp with built-in limitations and a blow-out point?
- Are we aware of them and their importance to our lives?
- Should we let these limitations govern our lives? What happens then?
- In a dire circumstance, has the plug ever been pulled on you? What happened then?
- If you believe God is the creator of the universe, what are the consequences if we do or do not observe and/or restrict our behavior in accordance with God's will as conveyed to us through Moses, the prophets, Jesus and scripture?

Responsibility

During the Covid-19 pandemic, numerous, unmasked protestors gathered together in public places insisting on their right to freely assemble without governmental restrictions. They know they are violating state and federal restrictions requiring people to self-quarantine in their homes and when running essential errands to wear face masks and to maintain a six-foot social distancing regulation. These protestors reject the advice of the medical care professionals and infectious disease experts. They claim that their First Amendment Rights in our nation's Bill of Rights are being violated by governmental regulations requiring them to wear face masks for the suppression of the Covid-19 pandemic.

Their reckless behavior endangers the lives of at least three others with whom they come in contact. Should they be held responsible for someone's infection and possible death? Are they carrying the virus to family members, friends, and associates? Are we not supposed to be our brother's keeper not the transmitter of Covid-19?

When the day comes that they contract this virus, let alone the number of people they may have infected, should the overworked medical profession treat them first or the innocent, law-abiding citizens who contracted Covid-19 through no fault of their own? Decisions like these have to be made daily in life.

Can we let the self-centered behavior of others sabotage our present and future well-being? In Matthew 25:1-13, Jesus compares admission to the kingdom of heaven by telling the parable of the wise and foolish maidens who took their lamps with them to meet the arriving bridegroom. The wise maidens took flasks of oil with them for their lamps. The foolish maidens did not. The bridegroom was delayed. When the foolish maidens realized they had no oil left, they asked the wise ones to give them some.

> But the wise replied, 'Perhaps there will not be enough for us and for you; go rather to the dealers and buy for yourselves.' And while they went to buy, the bridegroom came, and those who were ready went in with him to the marriage feast; and the door was shut. Afterward the other maidens came also, saying, 'Lord, lord, open to us.' But he replied, 'Truly, I say to you, I do not know you.' Watch therefore, for you know neither the day nor the hour. (Matthew 25:1-13)

Often unexpected burdens are thrust upon us. Sometimes we do not know how to resolve the dilemma of what we should do. What is our responsibility as God's children? Jesus' parable of the wise and foolish maidens reminds me of the Covid-19 protestors and others who go racing through life, grabbing what they can from others without any care or thought to the consequences of their actions. They always expect someone to bail them out of any trouble they might get themselves into as though all privileges and help are their due rather than a gift.

Plastered on many college administration offices is a sign that says: "Your poor planning does not constitute a crisis for me." The foolish maidens can be compared to carefree, freeloaders that exist in most societies. They go through life unprepared and take no responsibility for the consequences of their actions. God is the bridegroom in this parable. The foolish maidens are not ready or prepared for meeting God. They are expecting someone else to help save them. They expect God to let them into the bridal feast no matter what their behavior or excuses may be. But God shuts the door to the bridal feast for the unprepared and the unrepentant.

Likewise, we should not let our valuable energies and medical resources be directed toward helping those who refuse to take responsibility for their lives and their own behavior. Hysterics and irresponsibility on the part of some people is a way of controlling and manipulating others and making them responsible for the hysterical person's well-being and dependency.

Jesus told the parable of the wise and foolish maidens for His hearers either to accept or reject His message. He did not try to manipulate or be held responsible for other people's behavior and decisions.

We, too, cannot allow others control our behavior and our future through sabotage or hostage-like activities. Let me give you an example. After one of my parishioners had her hip replaced, I visited her in the hospital. The woman in the bed next to her refused to do anything to help herself. Her family stood by helplessly wringing their hands while the medical staff tried to motivate the sick woman into action. This sick woman had everybody exactly where she wanted them. Contrasted to her was my elderly parishioner walking around with discomfort and pain.

You see, we need to be able to separate legitimate needs such as incapacitation, mental and physical illness, from self-induced manufactured needs and their subsequent consequences. Also, we cannot do for others what they must learn to do for themselves. Otherwise we deprive them of their growth and independence. Motivation determines how we climb the hills and descend into the valleys of our lives.

Think About It

- During the Covid-19 pandemic, should unmasked demonstrators be allowed to gather together in a mass protest to assert their First Amendment rights? What makes you think so?
- What is their responsibility for protecting the vulnerable?
- Who should care for these demonstrators when they become ill with Covid-19?

Lost

Not so long ago while getting ready to take a shower, my doorbell rang. Not dressed to go to the door, I opened my second-floor bathroom window to find out who was there. A man probably in his sixties appeared. He said he was lost and wanted to know how to get to a certain highway which wasn't in the vicinity. I told him how he could get onto the nearby highway, that I did not know how he could get to his destination, and that he should look at his road map, and/or his GPS to help guide him. He had neither. So, he got into his car and probably drove to the nearby highway for which I gave directions. I doubt he ever reached his destination. Why?

Maybe he really wasn't lost and wanted to get access into my home. Maybe he had dementia. I can't imagine a person wanting to reach a certain unfamiliar destination without first checking a road map or a GPS on how to get there.

I wonder how many people live their lives without the wherewithal on how to travel the road of life. They may listen to anyone who will keep them stuck in a certain place that encourages a closed mind and lack of purpose in life. Is it laziness and/or lack of initiative and intelligence that causes people to get lost?

Enough! Unmask Sexual Predators

Be on guard so that your hearts are not weighed down with dissipation and drunkenness and the worries of this life, and that day catch you unexpectedly, like a trap. For it will come upon all who live on the face of the whole earth. Be alert at all times, praying that you may have the strength to escape all these things that will take place, and to stand before the Son of Man. (Luke 21:34-36)

Sexual predators cannot hide from God. They strike vulnerable men, women, and children with impunity mostly behind closed doors. In the past, fear and shame kept victims silent. Now the

#MeToo movement has emboldened women to speak out against sexual predators. Their bravery has helped to remove sexual predators from positions of power. Estimates run as high as one in six women have been sexually assaulted. Many of these women have stepped out of the shadows to tell their story and the long-term emotional, psychological, physical, and spiritual impact it has had upon them. Numbers are high for sexual assaults against men and children as well.

Historically and today, predators and sex offenders in positions of power try to discredit victims' testimonies. These predators get away with it often based on lack of evidence. Think about why this happens. Sexual predators do not assault their victims in public. That way they can deny it ever happened. Predators choose places and opportunities that cannot be verified by eyewitnesses. And women, for their part, do not want to be shamed and humiliated further by identifying their predator to law enforcement personnel knowing full well that their misfortune may not be believed.

When we get right down to it, *sin and self-centeredness* are at the heart of sexual predatory behavior. So what is sin? Christians and Jews believe that apart from God sin has no meaning. I like Old Testament Professor Walter Brueggemann's definition of God. He believes God is a holy power with a moral purpose that is non-negotiable.

In the Middle Ages, theologians identified and created a list of seven deadly sins they thought we needed to purge from our lives because they believed these sins entrap our souls and dehumanize us. These sins are

1. Greed
2. Sloth or apathy or avoidance of our obligations
3. Lust
4. Anger
5. Pride or self-centeredness

6. Envy
7. Gluttony

How many of these sins possess today's sexual predators?

Additionally, have these predators truly sought forgiveness? A trip to the confessional without true repentance is useless. The sinners are still separated from God. So what is repentance? True repentance is a turning away from sin and evil. It is a conversion and orientation to God. True repentance leads to a clean heart and a change in attitude and deeds.

Forgiveness for sins committed is conditional on the perpetrator

- Naming the sin committed,
- Accepting the blame for it,
- Sincere repentance and remorse,
- And, if possible, restitution for the victim.

"There is no cheap grace before God. Dietrich Bonhoeffer coined this term in his book *The Cost of Discipleship* (Colliers Books, 1963, 45, 47). He says: "Cheap grace is the grace we bestow on ourselves. Cheap grace is the preaching of forgiveness without requiring repentance, baptism without church discipline, communion without confession, absolution without personal confession. Cheap grace is grace without discipleship, grace without the cross, and grace without Jesus Christ."

Lack of repentance determines whether our eternal lives will be with God or barred from God's presence.

It is important for parents to gather as a family for extended educational discussions with their sons and daughters. For starters, young people need to be made aware of the dangerous effects of alcohol induced behavior and aggression, drug use, sex, peer pressure, the price for acceptance, and cliquish traditions and practices amongst peers as well as within fraternities and sororities. If you feel ill-prepared for such discussions, then find a professional who can discuss these issues with your children. Be open and available to your children. Remember that they have begun their physical, mental, emotional, and spiritual journey and need all the guidance they can get.

If they have not already done so, schools and universities need to establish, discuss, educate, and enforce rules of proper contact among their students and faculty. And houses of worship need to step up to the plate as well. What does God demand of all of us regarding the use and misuse of our bodies? As 2 Timothy 2:22 advises us, "Shun youthful passions and pursue righteousness, faith, love, and peace, along with those who call on the Lord from a pure heart."

As Edmund Burke once said, "All that is necessary for the triumph of evil is that good men do nothing."

Think About It

- Why do you agree or disagree with what I have written here?
- Have you or someone you know been sexually assaulted?
- How did you or they survive the assault?
- Were you or they intoxicated or high on drugs?

Rabbi Considers Sexual Misconduct and Repentance

Rabbi Danya Ruttenberg, rabbi-in-residence at Avodah, a Jewish social justice organization that deals with pressing issues facing this country, wrote an important article on September 6, 2018, in the *Washington Post*. The title of her piece is "Famous abusers seek easy forgiveness. Rosh Hashanah teaches us repentance is hard."

I think it will be helpful to Christians if they would consider the Jewish perspective on repentance and redemption. For this article, Ruttenberg focuses on famous men known for their sexual misconduct that removed them briefly from the public eye only to be restored a year or so later to their former positions. She asks, "Are these men sorry? Should they be forgiven? More to the point, perhaps, **who has the right to forgive them**?

Most non-Jews do not understand that there is no place for cheap grace and easy forgiveness as our pop culture accepts and expects, because they do not know the true meaning of repentance—"the work that a person who has done harm must undertake."

Repentance requires the sinner to publicly and sorrowfully own the harm he has done which also involves an inner struggle to make a change in his behavior so that he never sins again. He then directs his life towards God. Also, these sinners should seek to make restitution to their victims financially and/or with sincere and meaningful apology. It is not the victims' responsibility to forgive predators. Only God has the right to forgive them.

- Do you agree? Why?
- What should be done to sexual predators?
- Why is there no penalty for sexual predators such as castration that would work as a deterrent for them?

Think About It

- What situation has made it hard for you to forgive someone especially if he/she never asked for forgiveness?

- Do you have a thought process that has worked for you to forgive someone?
- Have you ever thought to turn the entire matter over to God and to move on?

Zero Sum Living

In the July 3, 2019, edition of *The Christian Century,* publisher Peter W. Marty wrote an article on *Zero-sum living.* Zero-sum game theory works on the basis that there must be winners and losers in this life of ours. He writes:

> The scorekeeping and power displays inherent in this win-or-lose approach are uninspiring at best and vengeful at worst. There's nothing lovely in thinking that my happiness requires someone else to be unhappy or that my appreciation for what I have in life depends on someone else having less.

Zero-sum living rears its head in our nation's political life, in sports, in immigration policies, in economics, in protection of our environment, etc. Most disconcerting is when it mixes with the gospel. Marty writes:

> Some Christians wonder what joy their salvation will bring if God saves everyone—as if joy in salvation depends on the misery of some people being damned. This kind of perverse zero-sum thinking has no place in the economy of God.

On the other hand, we must recognize that there will always be winners and losers in certain endeavors. Some people are more gifted as doctors, lawyers, scientists, mathematicians, manual laborers, artists, authors, musicians, and artists. Realizing one's limitations can be a good thing. Why try to be something you either have no interest in or no talents. We all learn to be resilient despite our loses and/or through our limitations. We learn by doing and hopefully be a contributing member of society.

Maya Angelou has two statements that should be considered. They are:

> I've learned that people will forget what you said. People will forget what you did. But people will never forget how you made them feel.
>
> You may not control all the events that happen to you, but you can decide not to be reduced by them.

Think About It

- Do you or your family live to win at all costs against your competitors? Why or why not?
- How does our society foster zero-sum living? Give some examples.
- Is there anything you can do to reverse a zero-sum living mentality? What might it be?
- If you are on the losing end of this mentality, what can you do to protect yourself yet foster love, kindness, grace, and charity towards others?

A Real Winner

Dear Grandson on your ninth birthday,

It seems you and your friends had a good time. When you told me that you placed only fourth out of ten in your contest, you seemed to suggest that you thought of yourself as less than a winner. Nothing could be further from the truth. Sometimes you win and sometimes you lose. It is how you live life that counts. A winner makes the best of any situation. That means that all winners put forth their best effort regardless of their placement in any competition.

The real test of a person's greatness is when he loves and cares for the non-winners. You will find in life that sometimes you will place first, fourth, eighth, and even in last place. That is O.K. as long as you put in your best effort and are a good person. Some winners think only of themselves and fail to help the needy. To me, they are selfish losers, not winners. Yet many winners are good people who do not seek self-glory or first place in everything. They are just putting forth their best effort.

Do you remember a few years ago when you were in Boston at Christmas time? You put all the money from your piggy bank into the Salvation Army's bucket? To my way of thinking you were a winner then. You showed us a better way. You helped the needy out of the goodness of your heart.

God loves those people who do God's will and who come to the aid of the poor and helpless. That is what Jesus taught us through his self-giving love. Winners have a grateful heart, a clear conscience, and a heart full of love. Their actions speak louder than words.

Love,
Grandma

Falling Leaves

I watch in wonder the beautiful autumn display of leaves on deciduous trees and bushes. Adequate weather conditions such as rain and sun as well as chemicals such a chlorophyll determine a leaf's health, color, and life span. Most leaves have their moment of glory before they free themselves from their parent and are carried by the wind and rain to new destinations. By doing so they make room for the next generation.

- Do you think our life's purpose may be to provide others with shade and protection from summer's scorching sun and worldly problems?
- What makes you think so?
- Where will the wind blow you to your final resting place?

29

WOUNDED HEALERS

How SHOULD we respond to the diseases, viruses, and other contagions that live in our environment? And what is the cost to others and ourselves?

Let's begin with Stephen R. Donaldson's character Thomas Covenant in *Lord Foul's Bane*. Thomas has been diagnosed with leprosy. It can be contagious through droplets coming from him similar to today's coronavirus spread. Thomas' doctors told him and his community in which he lives that his leprosy is not of the contagious kind. Yet the community fears catching his leprosy which dominates their actions toward him.

The narrative opens with Thomas Covenant walking into town to pay his electric bill. Everyone avoids him. He could have mailed his check to the electric company. But he had learned to see that act as a surrender, an abdication to the mounting ostracism practiced against him. People had been paying his bills and sending him groceries without charging him so that he would not need to walk among them.

While Thomas was in treatment for his leprosy, his wife divorced him and took their son with her to another state. The divorce had been granted because no compassionate law could force a woman to raise her child in the home of a man with leprosy.

I often wonder how people handle rejection when there is absolutely no hope of ever, ever being accepted again into human society because they have a communicable disease.

Let me tell you how Ken, an AIDS patient dealt with his isolation. Ken had accepted his death sentence. That alone was difficult, but Ken has found something even more difficult. He said:

> What is really bad is that you are considered condemned property. People look at you as someone who has done a great evil and is now being punished by God. And since AIDS is so deadly, people avoid touching me or anything I touch even though AIDS is only transmitted through bodily functions and not touch. People even avoid looking at me—as if looking might itself be contagious!

After a dreadful night of little or no sleep and a great deal of discomfort, Ken broke down and cried. He felt so terribly alone and afraid. There was no healing, no help until a very special nurse named Nancy saw him that morning. She walked over to Ken's bed and hugged him. He cried and cried, but she continued to hold him.

"You don't know what that did to me," he said later. "No one touches AIDS patients. Do you know how long it has been since someone has touched me? Really touched me?"

There was healing in Nurse Nancy's touch, very much like the healing the hemorrhaging woman experienced when she touched Jesus' garment. (Mark 5:28-34) The laws of her society said that she must have sinned in some awful way to be burdened with her physical ailment. As an outcast, she must have had a terrible sense of isolation. At first, the woman's desire to touch Jesus' garment may have been her belief that His garments had healing powers. But Jesus does not let her leave with this misunderstanding. He asks, "Who touched me?" This woman shows integrity and courage by stepping forward. Jesus does not rebuke her stealth and perhaps her spiritual immaturity. He takes her where he finds her and helps her to grow spiritually. After hearing her story, Jesus does not judge her. He tells her that it is her faith, not His garments that made her well. Then Jesus says, "Go in peace and be restored to wholeness and salvation. Your faith has saved you."

Likewise, there was healing in Nurse Nancy's touch, very much like the healing in Jesus' interactions with the woman who was hemorrhaging. Ken was not physically healed. But there was a healing—a spiritual healing—that comes from compassionate human touch.

In all of the stories about Jesus' miracles, Jesus makes contact with human beings. He touches their lives with radical change. Rarely do we know the conclusion of these people's lives. But faith in Jesus opens new possibilities for recovery and a life of Christian discipleship.

Jesus sets the pattern. He starts with people where they are. He does not judge them. He heals them body and soul by being willing to help them. This is what we in the Christian church should be about. At its best, the Christian church on earth is an extension of Jesus' presence in the world.

With all its imperfections, sins, blemishes, and warts, the Christian church is the intended healer of the world's wounds. Christians are called to be compassionate healers. Compassion means entering into other people's lives. It means shouldering their burdens. It means standing in their shoes.

The great illusion of leadership is to think that we can be led out of the desert by someone who has never been there. The world needs healers who have suffered themselves. These wounded healers are willing to pay the price in helping them.

Wounded healers are aware of the loneliness of suffering because they have been there.

People who suffer long to be touched by people who really care, people who are not afraid to show tenderness and compassion. When a person feels that he or she is on death's door, the touch, the feel of another person's hand on them tells them that someone still cares for them, that they are not suffering alone. No words need be spoken.

Jesus was a healer. And we in the church are called to be like Him. We are to touch the lives of other people. All our actions should be born of God. We are to share our good fortune with those less fortunate than ourselves. We need to help those who are hurting and in need within our own country, at our borders, in refugee camps, and those seeking asylum from violence, war, and predators. Many refugee organizations have stepped up to help the needy especially in war-torn countries. Many churches have become sanctuaries for asylum seekers in the United States.

Think About It

Our lives have their many temptations that can pull us down the swollen river of life.

- Will you let that river drown you?
- Will you get in a boat to help save those who are drowning?
- Can you or are you a wounded healer?
- What do you think God wants you to be and do?
- Does everything stop with you?

Could it be that life's true destination is to help the needy and to bless others with our touch?

30

THE GIFT OF LIFE

NOTHING IS MORE adorable than a newborn baby especially when the child is our own. As proud parents, we start to plan a successful pathway into the future for our baby. The possibilities are unlimited.

When Mary accepts God's invitation to be the mother of Jesus, she is overjoyed with thoughts of greatness for herself and for Jesus. The visits of the shepherds only reinforce these beliefs. But Mary soon learns when she presents the baby Jesus in the Temple that her dreams are a mirage. Simeon, an old man who believed he would not see death until he had seen the Lord's Messiah, takes Jesus into his arms and thanks God for letting him see the salvation of the world. Then he says to Mary, "This child is destined for the falling and the rising of many in Israel, and to be a sign that will be opposed so that the inner thoughts of many will be revealed—and a sword will pierce your own soul too." (Luke 2:34-35)

No mother, however insensitive, wants to hear the future of her precious child to be tragic. Yet Jesus is a gift to her and to the world. Among the many gifts we give to each other at Christmas, the most important one is the gift of Jesus. Many do not open or accept this gift. Why?

During World War II, a name was coined by French doctors for a disease that made its appearance in prison camps. They called it "barbed-wire sickness." One of its symptoms was an appalling sense of futility and meaninglessness of existence. For many, this barbed-wire sickness affects the human spirit today. The source for it is the loss of the perspective and the dimension of the eternal. Life is closed in on itself.

People living in ghettos and/or refugee camps often exhibit symptoms of barbed-wire sickness. Some people have no hope, no energy, and insufficient education to enable them to get themselves out of their present prison. Others escape by joining cults, terrorists' groups, hate and white supremacy groups that seem to give them meaning, purpose and direction for their lives.

Some well-off citizens suffer this sickness, too. They become obsessed with money and possessions. This self-imposed barbed-wire sickness was captured by Charles Dickens in his character Scrooge whose purpose in life was the accumulation of wealth. In this process of building his wealth, he built a prison for himself. Scrooge shut God and others out of his heart and out of his life. He turned into a miserly, pathetic creature. All of his actions were governed by the question: "What's in it for me?"

It is interesting to discover that people in the Old and New Testament generally have this same attitude—what's in it for me? If I favor God with my love and devotion, what will I get in return? They were taken aback, as are we, when we discover that God is calling us to be Jesus' disciples and to continue His work "to bring good news to the poor, to proclaim release to the captives and recovery of sight to the blind, and to let the oppressed go free." (Luke 4:18)

Jesus came to redeem the world. He deals with our souls and pride. He wants to conquer the evil that exists in our hearts and minds. He highlights the differences between the material and spiritual world. Love of the material world separates people from each other and from God. Love of God brings people into communion with God and each other.

Jesus is Emmanuel—God with us. God's incarnate entrance into our world is as a human baby. Babies are the most helpless of all God's creatures and the most dependent on others for care and survival. God comes to us in love and in total vulnerability. God is telling us that God refuses to use His power to dominate us and to force his love upon us and to expect reciprocal love in return.

Jesus once said that "Foxes have holes, and birds of the air have nests, but the Son of Man has nowhere to lay his head." (Luke 9:58) Perhaps what Jesus wants us to learn is that the world is a transient place, a temporary residence. Life in this world is a continual round of birth and death. Jesus' birth signals the end of one era of time and the beginning of another. Yet, if we take even a superficial look at our society, we wonder whether Jesus' birth has had any lasting impact on it. Historically, it has. Human life and needs are valued by our society. But today, we are experiencing changing moral values, declining spiritual beliefs, and shifting ideas about the worth of human life. Much of life has become anchorless and rudderless. We are cast adrift.

I suggest that we should not be discouraged about the age we live in. Our times are also times of great opportunity for God's people. The time has come for people to find out what life is all about by becoming Jesus' disciples, by adding a vertical dimension to their lives, and by overcoming any barbed-wire sickness that robs the spirit of its eternal dimension.

We are invited into Jesus' world and are expected to continue His work in the world.

Think About It

- Do you know anyone with barbwire sickness?
- What can you do to help that person?

31

TRUST

Is it possible to have belief in the risen Jesus if you have not seen Him? The gospel of John is believed to have been written between 90-120 CE addresses this question.

Most all who knew Jesus were now dead. Christian persecutions were commonplace. Non-believers scoffed and ridiculed Christians for their belief in a risen Jesus. They would pointedly ridicule believers by saying:

Can you believe that that Christian over there believes that a man crucified on a cross rose from the dead? Hah! Hah! What a fool!

Doubt entered Christian thoughts. Was their belief all a farce? In John 20:19-29, Thomas is used as a foil to help those Christians experiencing a crisis in their belief. Thomas is experiencing the age-old dilemma as to whether we have to touch or scientifically verify someone or something in order to believe in someone or something.

The scene of this story opens shortly after Jesus' resurrection. The disciples are huddled in fear behind locked doors. They are disillusioned, leaderless, and frightened. Then Jesus appears to them. Thomas, however, is not present. When he hears the disciples' fantastic story, he doubts them. Thomas is a sceptic and wants physical evidence on which to base his belief in their claims. After all, had not God abandoned Jesus on the cross? Why then would God raise Jesus from the dead? No one had ever been resurrected from the dead before. Jesus' disciples were just imagining the impossible.

Eight days later, Jesus returns. He greets them and turns to Thomas. Thomas "put your finger here, and see my hands; and put out your hand, and place it in my side; do not be faithless, but believing." Thomas' doubt turns to certainty and belief. "My Lord and my God!" These particular titles belong only to God. Thomas sees Jesus as being more than Israel's Messiah. He now understands that Jesus is the clearest revelation of God that God has given to the world. The doctrine of the Trinity had not been clarified at this time by the early Christians. Yet Thomas partially understands it and addresses Jesus as "My Lord and my God!"

Jesus replies:

> Have you believed because you have seen me? Blessed are those who have not seen and yet believe.

Thomas' experience is the early church's answer to their crisis in belief. Doubt often is a prerequisite to belief. Today our doubts are just as real as they were for Thomas. Jesus is not physically present to us. Nor do we know anyone to whom Jesus has been physically present. We want a reasonable belief that is compatible with the everyday world we experience.

To help us in our unbelief, we must rely on the New Testament scripture, history, and the witness of the Christian community. How trustworthy are these three sources?

History verifies the existence, crucifixion and death of Jesus. Jesus had a human body. He died as all humans die. But history cannot verify the resurrection. All that we can know is that Jesus made some post-resurrection appearances. And for this knowledge, we have to rely solely on the words of the witnesses.

The New Testament is the early church's written witness of Jesus Christ and of the formation of the Christian church. From the New Testament **scripture,** we can learn how Jesus trusted in God. We learn that Jesus lived by two principles. They are complete obedience to God and total self-giving. Jesus submits only to God's authority. He swears no allegiance to anyone or anything. He remained true to His calling and became a bright light and a source of hope to those living in a dark and hopeless world. He showed us an alternate way of living through obedience to God and self-giving. He did not run from the cross. If He had, His entire ministry would be a self-contradiction.

On the cross, Jesus showed us that God shares our humanity and suffers with us. God is more than some distant, transcendental God. God is here with us. When death came to Jesus, He ended his perishable human form of existence and entered into an imperishable existence. Jesus trusted in God to the very end, even unto death. God validated Jesus' life and death through Jesus' resurrection. We who respond to God in Christ will pass as Jesus did from death to a new life. For this reason, Jesus' death and resurrection are telling us that we should not fear death. All of us are finite and will die. But our lives will extend beyond our present mortality into immortality.

Jesus' disciples are His first **witnesses.** Jesus will not let them isolate themselves from the rest of the world. They are ordered out into the world to witness to the world God's redeeming and reconciling love.

> Go therefore and make disciples of all nations, baptizing them
> in the name of the father and of the Son and of the Holy Spirit,
> teaching them to observed all that I have commanded you; and

lo, I am with you always, to the close of the age. (Matthew 28:19-20)

These once bungling, fearful disciples, with the aid of God's spirit, start the Christian movement which eventually overtook most of the Roman Empire. Their witness was believed and passed on from one generation to another generation through the Christian community. Jesus becomes known to each generation through those who believe in Him.

But we must be selective as to which Christian witness we will trust. The Christian church has had and continues to experience clerical misconduct and corruption, superstition, rivalry, heresies, and numerous other distortions all in the name of Jesus Christ. And for the past several decades, we have had the multi-million dollar business of TV evangelism. Frankly, with all the religious and theological hype bombarding us daily, I can understand why many are confused and either distrust, reject, or mock Christianity.

Whom then can we trust? Only God. But how do we learn about God? We cannot touch, see, or hear God? We can and do experience God's presence at certain special moments in our lives.

It is through the witnessing Christian community which experiences God's presence in it that we learn about God. This community also studies and lives according to the Holy Scripture. Like Thomas, our honest doubts, questioning, and searching help us seek answers. God is hidden to us and is only partially revealed to us through the prophets, Jesus Christ, scripture, and those people who witness to God daily. There are no easy solutions to our quest.

Jesus trusted God to the very end even though He felt abandoned and forsaken by God. We, too, need to have that same trust. God has bestowed His grace on us to be used by us for our spiritual growth. Learn about God by studying your Bibles, attending worship, and from honest Christian witnesses.

One such Christian witness during World War II was Dietrich Bonhoeffer. He dared to fulfill his vows as a Lutheran minister. He challenged the corruption of the Nazis regime. He could have turned his head in another direction. He did not have to be so outspoken against the evil he saw. He could have stayed in America where he was safe and not have returned to Germany. He could have rationalized, as most of the world did, that the Nazis were putting food on people's tables, prosperity was returning to Germany, and that the majority were benefitting. Only the scapegoats such as the Jews were suffering.

Bonhoeffer's trust in God and God's demands on him in this world to be an honest Christian witness against the evils he saw caused him to raise his voice in dissent. He did not run from his responsibility, from his cross. Instead he was imprisoned and eventually executed by the Gestapo.

Another Christian witness was Mother Teresa who died in 1977 at the age of 87. She worked the streets of Calcutta where over 50,000 people at that time were homeless and lived on the streets. She and her sisters lived a selfless commitment to God by working and caring for the dying, the unwanted, the orphans, the lepers, and the abandoned. She believed that life comes from God. Life is sacred. These homeless are God's challenge to us. She said:

> The worst sickness, which no medicine can ever heal, is the feeling of being unwanted and abandoned. The greatest evil in the world is indifference towards people, lying in the street— exploited, poor and sick.

A third Christian witness to the risen Christ is Corrie ten Boom, a concentration camp victim. She writes in one of her books about

Meeting the guard from the concentration camp where she and her family had been held by the Nazis. She had been speaking at a large church meeting. After the meeting, the guard from the camp came forward. He put out his hand to her, and she instinctively pulled back, remembering the horrors to which that hand had been put or in which it had cooperated. But then she testified: 'Something came over me. I knew not what. I reached out and grasped his hand and extended my forgiveness as the tears rolled down his cheeks.... I only know that to forgive in such a manner is beyond human comprehension. It is the work of God and can only be done by us through the grace of God at work in us.'

Corrie ten Boom received the grace to forgive in the moment the grace was needed, and not before. Forgiveness like the resurrection, breaks in upon us through shut doors, and we do not know how it happens.

There are millions of unknown and unsung Christian witnesses who live ordinary lives. They are the people who bring joy and happiness to a shut in, inspiration to discouraged people, and hope to those who have forgotten Jesus' message and triumph over death through His resurrection.

Like Thomas, you may ask how trustworthy are these witnesses? Have they really experienced the transforming power of Jesus without seeing or touching Jesus? Only you can answer those questions.

If you do not trust these Christian witnesses, then whom or what do you trust? And historically how reliable are the things or persons in whom you put your trust?

Can you say as Thomas did, "My Lord and my God."

32

WHY JESUS IS CALLED THE SUFFERING SERVANT

He was despised and rejected by men;
A man of sorrows, and acquainted with grief
Surely he has borne our griefs and carried our sorrows;
Yet we esteemed him stricken, smitten by God, and afflicted.
But he was wounded for our transgressions...
With his stripes we are healed. (Isaiah 53)

MARK 8:27-38 uses the image of the Suffering Servant found in Isaiah 53 as a major theme for Jesus' ministry. These passages of the Suffering Servant were written some 500-600 years before Jesus. Old Testament Jews viewed sin as a condition of dreadful separation from God. God was their sole source for well-being. Apart from God, people were considered lost, unable to find themselves or find true happiness. Cultic rituals and Jewish legalism were religious attempts at atonement, at finding oneness with God. For some, these attempts were useless. They believed that only God could bring them deliverance and back into a relationship with God.

The New Testament view of sin appears to be even more grievous than the Old Testament view and thereby increases the value of Jesus' gift of salvation through His death and resurrection.

Early Christians believed suffering as the great purifier when it was accepted without bitterness. Isaiah's Suffering Servant encountered and accepted suffering as part of his work. His suffering became the means whereby he accomplished his work. It was effective in the salvation of others. Isaiah showed how the Suffering Servant vicariously assumes the punishment for his nation. The primitive Christian church adopted these Old Testament views of suffering and atonement in their effort to vindicate Jesus' ministry and death.

Who among us really wants to be a Suffering Servant? Being rejected and despised by others is a grim picture of human existence. We want to be loved or at least liked by most people who know us. Some of us even want to seek fame and fortune. Being despised runs against the human grain. Often we learn through the media about suicides of those who felt rejected and despised. Those who knew these suicidal people are overwhelmed with guilt and grief. They feel if only they had said or done something nice to that person so that person would not have taken his/her life. Being rejected, despised, and shunned by people is an unbearable, tragic role to bear in life.

In his gospel, Mark is attempting to combat a belief in Jesus that emphasizes His power and glory rather than His suffering and rejection by the power brokers in Israel namely the Pharisees, Sadducees, and the Herodians. Mark emphasizes a Christology based on the necessity for Christ's suffering and the necessity for His followers to follow in Jesus' steps through suffering, death, and ultimately to resurrection and glory. Most people disagree with Mark. They say that Jesus' way is not their way.

Mark deliberately structures his gospel with a picture of Jesus' self-understanding in terms of Isaiah's Suffering Servant.

Mark believes Jesus is the fulfillment of Isaiah's prophecy. Mark 10:45 describes Jesus' entire life when he writes, "The Son of Man also came not to be served but to serve, and to give His life as a ransom for many."

Mark drew heavily on the Old Testament scripture. Without it, Christians would have found it almost impossible to explain Jesus or the meaning of His life, death and resurrection. It was the Old Testament that enabled the Christian community to identify itself as the New Israel.

Dr. Brevard Childs, my Old Testament professor at Yale Divinity School, views the Old and the New Testaments as Partners in the Canon. Both testaments witness to God. He says:

> By reading the Old Testament along with the New as Christian scripture, a new theological context is formed for understanding both parts which differs from hearing each Testament in isolation. The Old Testament is interpreted by the New, and the New is understood through the Old.

In effect, we must look at the message of the entire Bible first before considering separate passages if we are to truly interpret their meaning without distortion. A proper understanding of Mark's Suffering Servant can only have meaning if it is read in the context of Isaiah's Suffering Servant.

Up to the time when Jesus and His disciples are on their way to Caesarea Philippi, the disciples appear slow-witted and sometimes self-seeking. They are incapable of understanding who Jesus really is. All their understanding will grow from the perspective of the cross and Jesus' resurrection. It is only after these events take place and the disciples have time to reflect on those events will the disciples be able to figure out their real meaning. Their knowledge and understanding will grow with time. Similarly, our knowledge and understanding of God grows through our life experiences, study of scripture, and walk with Jesus.

When Jesus asks Peter, "But who do you say that I am?" and Peter answers, "You are the Christ." Peter only dimly recognizes who Jesus is. We know this by Peter's reaction to Jesus' telling His stunned disciples that the Son of Man will suffer many things, be rejected by the religious establishment and be killed.

How can this be? Is not Jesus the Christ? Peter has the audacity to take Jesus aside and rebuke Jesus for entertaining such thoughts. Peter cannot accept the Suffering Servant role for Jesus. It is too awful, too degrading. It will serve no purpose. It is not the glory train that a Messiah or the Christ should have.

So what does it mean to be a disciple of Jesus? His invitation to us is in the shadow of the cross with a starkness and harshness that is almost too much for us to bear. Followers will not live an enraptured existence. In Mark, Jesus' demand on His disciples will be the same demand He puts on Himself, the way of the cross. Jesus asks nothing of us He does not ask of Himself. He came to awaken within our souls the greatness we can achieve if we learn to say "No" to ourselves and "Yes" to God. He wants us to say "No" to every course of action based on self-seeking and self-will. He wants us to say humbly that God has a place in our hearts. We are to be Jesus' lowly servants. All glory will come beyond the grave. Every act of kindness we do should be an expression of sympathy with Jesus and not something to bring acclaim to ourselves. The path to the cross is one of service and humiliation.

William Barclay gives a good example of one who dies to self. A monk called Telemachus lived in the latter half of the fourth century. He left the world, went into the desert to live alone in prayer, meditation, and fasting so as to save his soul.

But somehow he felt there was something wrong. One day as he rose from his knees, it suddenly dawned upon him that his life was based, not on a selfless love of God, but on a selfish love of God. It came to him that if he were to serve God he must serve people and that the desert was no place for a Christian to live, that the cities were full of sin and therefore full of need.

Telemachus set out for Rome. Most of the Roman world had been Christianized even though gladiatorial games still existed and were now frequented by Christians. In the arena, Christians were replaced by war prisoners. When Telemachus reached Rome, a victory celebration was going on.

Telemachus found his way to the gladiatorial arena. There were about 80,000 people there. The chariot races were ending; and there was a tenseness in the crowd as the gladiators prepared to fight. Into the arena they came with their greeting, "Hail, Caesar! We who are about to die salute you!" The fight was on and Telemachus was appalled. Men for whom Christ had died were killing each other to amuse an allegedly Christian populace. He leapt the barrier. He was in between the gladiators, and for a moment they stopped. "Let the games go on," roared the crowd. They pushed the old man aside; he was still in his hermit's robes. Again he came between them. The crowd began to hurl stones at him; they urged the gladiators to kill him and get him out of the way. The commander of the games gave an order; a gladiator's sword rose and flashed; and Telemachus lay dead.

Suddenly the crowd was silent. They were shocked that a holy man should have been killed in such a way. There was a mass realization of what this killing really was. The games ended abruptly that day—and they never began again. Telemachus by dying, had ended them.... "His death was more useful to people than his life." By losing his life he had done more than ever he could have done in lonely devotion in the desert.

The very essence of a Christian life is risking and spending our lives in God's service. We can never possess our own life. If we try, we will lose it. As disciples of Christ, we have only one option in our one lifetime. We are to respond to Jesus' invitation to follow after Him no matter what the cost. We are to love one another, repay no one evil for evil, and return good for evil. We are to be peacemakers.

Repentance and forgiveness require a change in our behavior. Jesus Christ's sacrifice does not provide us with cheap grace from God. Jesus' sacrifice requires us to know, love, and obey our Lord. And we are to make reparations for the evil we have done. Jesus asks us today to rethink our journey in life and whether it will bring us to our destination of eternal union with God.

Think About It

- What makes you believe or disbelieve that Jesus is a Suffering Servant?
- How were lives changed by Telemachus' death?
- What do you think is the difference between a selfless love for God and a selfish love of God?
- Is isolation from the world the answer to the needs of God's people? What makes you think so?

AFTERWORD

Thank you for letting me share my thoughts, doubts, questions, and struggles that I have experienced on my Christian journey. It has not always been easy to trust and believe in an unseen God. It is my hope that this book has helped you to turn the key and open the door to an enriched life of faith that will engage your critical thinking as you too struggle with your spiritual growth, doubts, and understandings that lead to a more mature faith.

I live on a dead-end street. When I drive my car to the bottom of my driveway, I can either make a left-hand turn towards the dead end or a right-hand turn that allows me to drive anywhere I want. My choice as in life is to accept the challenge of an open road that gives me the freedom to explore new possibilities, to meet with family and friends, and to preach and teach other people of the endless hope we have in Jesus Christ and His teachings.

I plan to write at least two or three more *Mustard Seed Thoughts* books which I hope will encourage and enlighten your spiritual growth. Visit my website www.mustardseedseries.com to let me know if you have any questions you wish me to cover. You can leave your questions through the Contact button. Also, let me know if you want to receive notification when the next book will be available. A review from you on Amazon and other places may be of help to others on their spiritual journey. My books also make good gifts for family and friends.

Let me leave you with a prayer I have prayed over the years. I am not sure who wrote it and/or whether I adopted and redid the prayer. It goes as follows.

> Go now with God.
> Be not tempted to stay in the safety of known places.
> Be not tempted to go only in your time.
> Elect not to go alone.
> Choose to go with God.
> Go in the faith that there is no valley so low,
> No wilderness so vast,
> No passage so crooked,
> No way so confused
> That God is not already there waiting to be with
> you. Amen

Made in the USA
Columbia, SC
02 October 2021

46085308R00111